DA...

At T...
Portsm...
T4800 was ready for its 236 Squadron crew, Flt Lt A K Gatward RCAF and observer Sgt G Fern. They were to make a low-level sortie, initially across Normandy. Two special pieces of 'ordnance' were on board – weighted French tricolore flags. In the lead-up to Bastille Day, they made a spectacular arrival in Paris flying down the Champs-Élysées, dropping a flag close to Napoleon's Arc de Triomphe. As 'C-for-Charlie' careered on along the avenue, the Kriegsmarine Headquarters in the Place de la Concorde filled Gatward's gunsight. Four 20mm cannon raked the building – Coastal Command had left an indelible 'calling card'! As the Beaufighter streaked overhead another tricolore was dropped. Gatward and Fern received a DFC and a DFM respectively for their exploit. (More of 236 Squadron in the feature 'Strike Wing' inside.)

Artist Mark Postlethwaite GAvA has portrayed the event superbly, depicting T4800 dropping a flag over the Champs-Élysées with the Eiffel Tower to the south, on the other side of the River Seine. Mark has an excellent web-site providing details of prints, giclées, originals and commissions – take a look at **www.posart.com**

6 CLOSE SHAVE
Andrew Thomas relates an encounter between a Beaufighter and an Fw 190 off the coast of Norway

10 'ACES'
A directory of those pilots who achieved five or more victories on 'Beaus', compiled by Andrew Thomas

14 ADAPT, IMPROVE, EXCEL
Some of the greatest warplanes started life as stop-gaps. M L Wynch describes the evolution of the Beaufighter

24 POWER
'Two engines hotly pursued by an airframe' was a tongue-in-cheek description of the increasingly potent Beaufighter. The four powerplants that drove the mighty 'Beau' are detailed

28 SQUADRON DIRECTORY
Andrew Thomas chronicles the units that flew the 'Beau'

34 MALTA'S AUXILIARIES
Robin J Brooks describes 600 'City of London' Squadron's brief, but decisive deployment to the George Cross Island

38 A LONDON 'BEAU'
Pete West profiles a war-weary 'City of London' night-fighter

40 RARE BIRDS
Considering its illustrious combat service, it is a pity that so few Beaufighters are extant

44 WHISPERING DEATH
Jim Grant details the exploits of Australian Beaufighters in the struggle against the Japanese

52 UNDER OTHER FLAGS
Doug Hall outlines overseas use of the Beaufighter and post-war exports

55 GOT SHARP EYES?
How good is your aircraft recognition?

56 PUNCH
In 1941 the Beaufighter was the most heavily armed fighter anywhere. We present a portfolio of its formidable arsenal

60 A BOB'S WORTH
A small booklet published in 1944 paid tribute to an aircraft the public were not that familiar with. Jonathan Garraway treasures his copy

62 STRIKE WING
After a faltering start, North Coates proved the Beaufighter to be a lethal anti-shipping weapon, as Graham Pitchfork explains

70 DESERTS AND SEAS
Convoy escort and anti-shipping strikes were just a part of 252 Squadron's repertoire, as Jonathan Garraway relates

80 STARS AND STRIPES
The Americans came to appreciate the qualities of the Beaufighter in the skies of the Mediterranean. Warren E Thompson chronicles the achievements of the 417th NFS

86 NIGHT OWLS
Andrew Thomas describes some of the exploits of Beaufighter night-fighters

92 TUGGING AT SLEEVES
The Beaufighter refused to retire; Doug Hall examines its second career, which lasted until 1960

ORIGINALLY PUBLISHED 2012
EDITOR: Ken Ellis
With thanks to: Steve Beebee, Julie Lawson, Nigel Price, Glenn Sands and especially Leslie George Frise

CHIEF DESIGNER: Steve Donovan
DESIGN: Lee Howson, Chris Abrams, Dave Robinson, Jigowatt Media
SENIOR EDITOR, SPECIALS: Roger Mortimer
EMAIL: roger.mortimer@keypublishing.com
COVER DESIGN: Dan Hilliard
ADVERTISING MANAGER: Brodie Baxter
EMAIL: brodie.baxter@keypublishing.com
TEL: 01780 755131
ADVERTISING PRODUCTION: Debi McGowan
EMAIL: debi.mcgowan@keypublishing.com

SUBSCRIPTION/MAIL ORDER
Key Publishing Ltd, PO Box 300, Stamford, Lincs, PE9 1NA
TEL: 01780 480404
SUBSCRIPTIONS EMAIL: subs@keypublishing.com
MAIL ORDER EMAIL: orders@keypublishing.com
WEBSITE: www.keypublishing.com/shop

PUBLISHING
GROUP CEO AND PUBLISHER: Adrian Cox
PUBLISHED BY
Key Publishing Ltd, PO Box 100, Stamford, Lincs, PE9 1XQ
TEL: 01780 755131 Website: www.keypublishing.com

PRINTING
Precision Colour Printing Ltd, Haldane, Halesfield 1, Telford, Shropshire. TF7 4QQ

DISTRIBUTION
Seymour Distribution Ltd, 2 Poultry Avenue, London, EC1A 9PU
ENQUIRIES LINE: 02074 294000.

We are unable to guarantee the bona fides of any of our advertisers. Readers are strongly recommended to take their own precautions before parting with any information or item of value, including, but not limited to money, manuscripts, photographs, or personal information in response to any advertisements within this publication.

© Key Publishing Ltd 2023

All rights reserved. No part of this magazine may be reproduced or transmitted in any form by any means, electronic or mechanical, including photocopying, recording or by any information storage and retrieval system, without prior permission in writing from the copyright owner. Multiple copying of the contents of the magazine without prior written approval is not permitted.

FRONT COVER
The timeless artistry of Roy Cross graced the boxes of many Airfix kits, including the Beaufighter. A Beaufighter TF.X of 236 Squadron, part of the famed North Coates Strike Wing, at the point of release of its torpedo. The Beaufighter TF.X is available in Airfix range at 1:72 scale. With many thanks to Airfix – www.airfix.com

THIS PAGE:
Main image: With rocket rails and 'Invasion Stripes' TF.X NT950 of 236 Squadron, North Coates Strike Wing, banks away from the camera ship. This machine failed to return from an attack off the Dutch Coast on October 3, 1944.
Key – Gordon Swanborough collection

Left: TF.X NE355 of 404 Squadron RCAF, based at Davidstow Moor, Cornwall, 1944.
Pete West

Close Shave

ANDREW THOMAS RECOUNTS AN ENCOUNTER BETWEEN A BEAUFIGHTER AND AN FW 190 OFF THE COAST OF NORWAY

Above: Norwegian-based Fw 190s – a tenacious 1/JG5 pilot damaged Hilly's Beaufighter sufficiently to write it off.

Aubrey Hilliard after being commissioned shortly after the encounter with Josef Gruber.

Beaufighters by Christmas was the prospect for the personnel of 235 Squadron. Formed just after the start of World War Two in the 'coastal fighter' role, 235 was equipped with Bristol Blenheim IVfs, on shipping protection tasks. As promised, at the end of December 1940 some Beaufighters arrived, but it proved to be a false dawn as they were soon withdrawn.

It was not until December of the following year that 235 was eventually converted to the pugnacious Bristol. 'Home' for the unit had been bases in northern Scotland, as its main operating area was the northern reaches of the North Sea and the southern part of the Norwegian Sea.

Under the command of Wg Cdr G H B Hutchinson, 235 moved to Chivenor in the summer of 1942 where, in October, Sgt Aubrey Hilliard – nicknamed 'Hilly' – joined the unit after his flying training. He flew his early operations from the north Devon base but, in January 1943, moved with 235 *back* to Scotland at Leuchars, on the east coast near St Andrews. Hilly and his colleagues mounted patrols over some very inhospitable seas and up along the rugged coastline of German-

"CREWS SOMETIMES DISAPPEARED WITHOUT TRACE—AS MUCH THE VICTIMS OF WEATHER AS TO THE LUFTWAFFE."

Pilots of 235 Squadron – Hilly is seated on the left.

occupied Norway – sometimes as escort to Handley Page Hampden torpedo-bombers and other times on independent sweeps. Crews sometimes disappeared without trace: as much the victims of weather as to the Luftwaffe.

Providing fighter defence for Norway was the responsibility of Jagdgeschwader (JG5) Eismeer (*Ice Sea*) which had begun forming in early 1942. Its main strength was in the north and east, facing the Soviets around Murmansk and in Karelia – but I Gruppe (I/JG5), under Hauptmann Gerhardt von Wehren, was based at Stavanger's Sola airfield to counter RAF anti-shipping units including 235 Squadron. By January 1943, I/JG 5 and its three Staffeln flew the Focke-Wulf Fw 190A, under Staffelführers Obtl Gerd Senoner (1 Staffel - 1/JG5), Hptn Gerhardt Buchel (2 Staffel) and Ltn Max Endriss (3 Staffel), based around the coast at Sola, Lista, Kjevik and Herdla. During February, Hptn Gerhardt Wengel became the Gruppenkommandeur with Oblt Rudolf Muller as his adjutant.

AVOID AND SURVIVE

No.235 Squadron was tasked with escorting six Hampden torpedo-bombers of 455 Squadron RAAF in a dusk sweep off the Norwegian coast on March 3. Led by Wg Cdr Baird, the seven Beaufighters lifted off at 4pm. One of them, Mk.Ic T3295 *A-for-Able*, was flown by Hilliard, now a Flight Sergeant, with his observer, F/Sgt Jimmy Hoyle. Flying at only 500ft (152m) above the waves, the 'Beaus' had to orbit in a wide circle astern of the slower Hampdens.

Nearing the enemy coast at about 5.30pm in indifferent weather with low cloud and poor visibility, a solitary fighter was sighted. Hilly, a veteran of many 'ops', remembered the engagement many years later:

"On nearing the coast south of Stavanger, my position was the rear aircraft – 'tail end Charlie' – of the formation when my observer called: 'Enemy aircraft at 9 o'clock same level coming straight towards us.'

"I saw it, opened the throttles and turned towards him, to lessen his deflection. He pulled up and went past 200 yards to port and we recognised it as an Fw 190.

Below: Beaufighter Ic T3295 'A' at Arbroath on the morning of March 4 bearing the scars of battle. Although appearing to be relatively undamaged, it never flew again.

U-BOAT KILLER

Shortly after the encounter with the Fw 190, 'Hilly' Hilliard converted to de Havilland Mosquitos and, having been commissioned, was posted to join 618 Squadron. This unit had been specially formed in April 1943 to carry a smaller variant of Dr Barnes Wallis' bouncing bomb for an attack on the German battleship 'Tirpitz'. He practised low-level flying and attacks, but plans changed.

Hilly moved to 248 Squadron equipped with the so-called Tsetse Mosquito – the Mk XVIII armed with a 57mm cannon for anti-U-boat and shipping patrols. On March 25, 1944 he sank Oblt Teisler's U-976 off St Nazaire with another Mosquito. The same pair combined two days later to damage U-960, commanded by Oblt Gunther Heinrich – whom Aubrey was to meet 40 years later.

Hilliard also saw action with 248 Squadron, flying the Tsetse Mosquito XVIII fitted with a 57mm gun. S G Nunn

"At this stage the formation had turned south and was a long way off. The '190 continued in a port turn towards the north-east as I levelled out heading south-west. He came in again at 4 o'clock and started firing at a range of about 800 to 900 yards. I noticed he was using the usual 1-in-3 tracer bullets or cannon shells and I turned sharply to starboard in a steep turn towards him again. In no time he pulled up and passed to starboard, turning port."

AGILE AND FAST

"Everything was happening so damned quickly – the '190 was very manoeuvrable and extremely fast; my Beaufighter on the other hand was shuddering at 260 knots! I continued the turn to starboard heading west, carrying out 'corkscrew' action from between sea level to 500 to 700ft – and, as you can imagine, skipping the waves was hair-raising in itself, let alone being attacked by enemy aircraft. Many times I was low enough for his tracer to go over the top of me."

Hilliard's T3295 wore the short-lived colour scheme of white fuselage with camouflaged top surfaces. As luck would have it, this was the only one not fitted with a rear gun – some having a 0.303in Vickers gas-operated and others a belt-fed Browning, the latter being considered the better weapon.

Aubrey: "Jimmy, my observer, gave me good positions of where the Fw 190 was, and he flashed his Aldis lamp at him to mimic gun flashes! A few more attacks took place and each time I took evasive action, corkscrewing then turning towards the '190 to create turbulence for him and lessen his deflection. After each attack, I steep-turned west, getting further away from the enemy coast.

"The combat lasted for about seven minutes. He had hit me several times, including the starboard engine and wing. I saw the tracer go in, but I was unable to make an attack on him: he was too manoeuvrable and fast. I was therefore out to save ourselves."

WRITTEN OFF

After the Fw 190 had pulled away it was soon lost in the murk. Aubrey gingerly eased the damaged Beaufighter up to about 7,000ft, continually monitoring the suspect starboard engine and

Another of 235's Beaufighters, wearing the short-lived mainly white 'coastal' colour scheme, after a wheels-up landing.

glancing at the canopy release handle in case he had to ditch. In the gathering dusk he flew back to Scotland, with Jimmy navigating by dead reckoning as the radio set had been destroyed and they unable to receive emergency fixes.

They made landfall in the dark just south of Peterhead, and after a time Aubrey spotted a set of runway lights, putting down at 8.35pm. They landed without brakes at HMS *Condor*, the Fleet Air Arm station at Arbroath, and had to ground loop, coming to rest just in front of a massive post!

"Jimmy went to get transport and, while he was away, I examined my left foot which was *very* wet. I thought it had been nicked by a bullet or shrapnel, but it turned out to be sweat! The reason is, I suppose, that I had anticipated, with apprehension, that the starboard engine would fail, and I was 'at the ready' with my foot on the port rudder pedal to correct the obvious swing to the right."

The following morning Hilliard and Hoyle examined their battered Beaufighter which, with cannon holes in the fuselage, starboard engine and propeller, had been declared a write off. The Luftwaffe Fw 190 pilot had unknowingly achieved his objective.

Of the rest of the formation, Wg Cdr Baird had crash-landed with hydraulic damage. The aircraft of Plt Off Turner (*B-for-Baker*) and Fg Off Howlett (*J-for-Jig*) also landed at Arbroath while two others made it back to Leuchars. Fg Off H E Hallam and his observer, Plt Off G H Turner, were killed when their machine crashed into a hill near Montrose.

Stavanger-based 1/JG5 had spent March 3 flying a succession of convoy escort patrols. A little after 6pm, Fw Josef Gruber lifted off from Sola at the controls of Fw 190A-2 2132 *White 6* for another patrol to the west of Stavanger. At 6.32pm he was reported as encountering a number of enemy aircraft in the vicinity and, without doubt, was Aubrey's persistent assailant.

Shortly afterwards, several aircraft from 2/JG5 took off for a night operation but soon returned after encountering practically zero visibility. Before long it became clear that Josef Gruber had failed to return. Gruber had probably flown *White 6* into the sea in the failing light and bad weather as he approached the coast. Unaware he had destroyed a Beaufighter, and he may have damaged Wg Cdr Baird's aircraft, the cruel waters off Norway claimed another pilot missing in action.

> "...THE '190 WAS VERY MANOEUVRABLE AND EXTREMELY FAST – MY BEAUFIGHTER ON THE OTHER HAND WAS SHUDDERING AT 260 KNOTS!"

Above: **In his account, Hilly bemoaned the lack of a rear cupola gun as fitted to all of 235's other 'Beaus'!**
Mike Hodgson via Peter Green collection

Left: **Aubrey's tailor's bill for uniform after his commissioning – he was even charged 4/6d for his pilot's wings!**
All A H Hillard via author unless noted

Sqn Ldr A D Boyd, on the right, during his time with 600 Squadron in Italy, 1944.

'ACES'

ANDREW THOMAS PRESENTS A DIRECTORY OF PILOTS WHO ACHIEVED FIVE OR MORE VICTORIES ON 'BEAUS'

Wg Cdr J R D Braham (right) with his observer, Sqn Ldr 'Sticks' Gregory. Braham was the top-scoring Beaufighter 'ace'.

Entering service at the end of the Battle of Britain, the pugnacious Bristol Beaufighter was deployed in numbers by Fighter Command just in time for the start of the Luftwaffe's night 'Blitz' on Britain. Flown by specialised squadrons, several of them elite pre-war Auxiliary Air Force units, it was the first night-fighter to be equipped with airborne radar as standard.

It combined the ability to 'see' the enemy at night with speed and the devastating hitting power of four cannon and six machine-guns. The Beaufighter was largely responsible for the blunting of the Luftwaffe's night offensive and, in the early months of 1941, a large number of successful pilots flew the type.

Its range and striking power also led to Beaufighter's deployment by Coastal Command as a long-range fighter taking on enemy maritime bombers. This eventually led to its coastal strike role.

The Beaufighter was also quickly deployed overseas in night-fighter,

ABOUT THE TABLES

In the claims list, the first number shows the 'destroyed' followed by 'probable' and then 'damaged' claims; eg: 5 - 4 - 3. Single shared claims are shown as a fraction, thus: 5½. Multiple shared claims are shown in full: +4sh. The initials 'ftl' stand for 'forced to land'.

Those pilots with less than five victories are marked thus * and are shown because of their inclusion in the definitive reference *Aces High*, and where there may be doubt as to their actual scores. For completeness, V-1 'doodlebug' victories are noted.

Theatre decode: UK - United Kingdom and NW Europe; **ME** - North Africa, Mediterranean and Italy; **FE** - India and Burma; **SWP** - South West Pacific including Australia and the East Indies.

Wg Cdr John Cunningham (left) and Flt Lt Jimmy Rawnsley, 604 Squadron.

Name	Service	Sqn/s	'Beau' Claims	Total	Theatre(s)
Braham J R D	RAF	29, 51 OTU, 141	19 - 2 - 5	29 - 2 - 5	UK
Cunningham J	RAF	604	16 - 2 - 6	20 - 3 - 7	UK
Shipard M C	RAAF	68, 89	13 - 2 - 2	13 - 2 - 2	UK
Fumerton R C	RCAF	406, 89	13 - 0 - 1	14 - 0 - 1	UK, ME
Turnbull J H	RCAF	125, 600	12½ - 0 - 0	12½ - 0 - 0	UK, ME
Buchanan J K	RAF	272	10+3sh - 0 - 6½	10+3sh - 0 - 6½	ME
Downing A B	RAF	141, 600	12 - 0 - 0	12 - 0 - 0	UK
Hughes F D	RAF	125, 600	11½ - 0 - 0	18½ - 1 - 1	UK, ME
Crombie C A	RAAF	25, 89, 176	11 - 3 - 1	11 - 3 - 1	UK, ME, FE
Willson J E	RAF	219, 153	10 - 1 - 1	10 - 1 - 1	UK, ME
Read J A A	RAF	604, 89, 46, 108	10 - 1 - 0	10 - 1 - 0	UK, ME
Boyd A D McN	RAF	600, 219	10 - 0 - 0	10 - 0 - 0	UK, ME
Coate E E	RAAF	236, 272, 252, 227	9½ - 0 - 8	9½ - 0 - 8	UK, ME
Green C P	RAF	600, 125	9 - 2 - 1	11 - 3½ - 1	UK
Hodgkinson A J	RAF	219	9 - 1 - 2	12 - 1 - 5	UK
Topham J G	RAF	219	9 - 1 - 0	13 - 1 - 1	UK
Reeves N E	RAF	89	9 - 0 - 2	14 - 0 - 2	ME
Schmidt D W	RCAF	236, 227	8½ - 1 - 5½	8½ - 1 - 5½	UK, ME
Mansfeld M J	Czech	68	8½ - 0 - 2	8+2sh- 0 - 2 +2 V1	UK
Davison M M	RAF	46, 89, 108	8 - 1 - 1	12 - 1 - 1 +1 V1	ME
Mellersh R J L	RAF	29, 600	8 - 1 - 0	8 - 1 - 0 +39 V1	UK, ME
Crew E D	RAF	604	8 - 0 - 4	12½ - 0 - 5 +21 V1	UK
Watson A	RAF	272	6+2sh - 0 - 1	6+2sh - 0 - 1	ME
Rankin	RRAAF	236, 227, 272, 30 RAAF	4+4sh - 1 - 0	4+4sh - 1 - 0	UK,ME, SWP
Chisholm R A	RAF	604	7 - 1 - 1	9 - 1 - 1	UK
Coleman G B S	RAF	256, 456, 89, 46, 272, 600	7 - 1 - 1	7 - 1 - 1	UK, ME
Edwards H G	RAF	89, 108	7 - 0 - 2	7 - 0 - 2	ME
Pring A M O	RAF	125, 89, 176	7 - 0 - 2	7 - 0 - 2	UK, ME, FE
Daniel E G	RAF	89, 1435 Flt	7 - 0 - 1	7 - 0 - 1 +4 V1s	ME
Kinmonth M W	RAF	406, 89, 51 OTU	7 - 0 - 1	7 - 0 - 1	UK, ME
Horne A W	RAF	219, 255, 600	7 - 0 - 0	7 - 0 - 0	UK, ME
Riley W	RAF	252, 272	6½ - 0 - 1	9+3sh - 1 - 1	UK, ME
Hayton G L	RAF	89, 1435 Flt	6 - 2 - 2	6 - 2 - 4	ME
Pike T G	RAF	219	6 - 2 - 1	6- 2 - 1	UK
Aitken M	RAF	68, 46 (det)	6 - 1 - 2	14½ - 1 - 3	UK, ME
Pepper G	RAF	29	6 - 1 - 0	6 - 1 - 0	UK
Owen A J	RAF	600	6 - 0 - 2	15 - 1 - 3 +1 V1	ME
Bailey J R A	RAF	125, 600, 54 OTU, 45 NFS	6 - 0 - 1	6 - 0 - 2	UK, ME
Etherton J H	RAF	89, 176	6 - 0 - 1	6 - 0 - 3	ME, FE
Rayment K G	RAF	153	6 - 1 - 1	6 - 1 - 1 +1 V1	UK
Rees S W	RAAF	600	6 - 0 - 1	6 - 0 - 1	ME
Bretherton B A	RAAF	255, 5 OTU RAAF	6 - 0 - 0	8 - 0 - 0	ME
Gloster M J	RAF	456, 255	6 - 0 - 0	11 - 0 - 0	UK, ME
Stephenson L	RAF	141, 153	6 - 0 - 0	10 - 0 - 0	UK, ME
Phipps R T	RAF	272	5½ - -1 - 0	5½ - 1 - 0	ME
Modera J R S	RAF	227	3+3sh - -2 - 1½	3+3sh - 2 - 1½	ME
Bobek L	Czech	68	5 - 2 - 3	5 - 2 - 3	UK
Allen P F	RAF	68, 125	5 - 2 - 1	5 - 2 - 1	UK
Gunnis H H K	RAF	252; 603	5 - 2 - 1	5 - 2 - 1	ME
Meagher P E	RAF	211	5 - 2 - 1	10 - 2 - 1	FE
Kendall P S	RAF	255	5 - 1 - 2	8 - 1 - 2	UK, ME
Pleasance H P	RAF	25	5 - 1 - 2	5 - 1 - 2	UK
Greaves D H	RAF	68, 255	5 - 1 - 1	9 - 1 - 1	UK, ME
Shead H F W	RAF	68, 25, 89	5 - 1 - 0	5 - 1 - 0	UK, ME
Tuckwell G A	RAF	272	5 - 1 - 0	5 - 1 - 0	ME
Gordon R L	RAAF	31 RAAF	5 - 0 - 2	5 - 0 - 2	SWP
Mackenzie R M	RAF	141, 409, 89, 46, 227	5 - 0 - 2sh	5 - 0 - 2sh	ME

Name	Service	Sqn/s	'Beau' Claims	Total	Theatre(s)
Williamson P G K	RAF	153	5 - 0 - 1	9 - 0 - 1	ME
Keele B R	RAF	604	5 - 0 - 1	6 - 0 - 1	UK
Boardman H S	RAF	600, 153	5 - 0 - 1	5 - 0 - 1	ME
Geddes K I	RAF	604	5 - 0 - 1	5 - 0 - 1	UK
Spurgen A L M	RAAF	68, 89	5 - 0 - 1	5 - 0 - 1	UK, ME
Styles L H	RAF	219, 153, 600	5 - 0 - 1	5 - 0 - 1	UK, ME
Thompson D A	RAF	600	5 - 0 - 1	5 - 0 - 1	ME
White D	RAF	C R Flt, 39	5 - 0 - 1	5 - 0 - 1	ME
Butler R T	RAF	108, 46	5 - 0 - 1	5 - 0 - 1	ME
Newhouse P S	RAF	68, 600	5 - 0 - 0	5 - 0 - 0	UK, ME
Pain D S	RAF	68, 89	5 - 0 - 0	5 - 0 - 0	UK, ME
Paton D P	RAF	600	5 - 0 - 0	5 - 0 - 0	ME
Sage P C W	RAF	89, 46	5 - 0 - 0	5 - 0 - 0	ME
Smith A I	RCAF	252, 272	5 - 0 - 0	5 - 0 - 0	ME
Johnson C L	RAF	227	4½ - 0 - 0	4½ - 0 - 0	ME
Cartridge D L	RAF	248	2+3sh - 0 - 0	2+3sh - 0 - 0	UK, ME
Melville-Jackson G H	RAF	236, 272, 248	2+3sh - 0 - 0	2+3sh - 0 - 0	UK, ME
Watters J	RAF	272, 603	2+6sh - 0 - ½	2+6sh - 0 - ½	ME
Joll I K S*	RAF	604	4 - 0 - 2	4 - 0 - 2	UK
Morris D G *	RAF	406	4 - 0 - 1	4 - 0 - 1	UK
Player J H *	RAF	255	4 - 0 - 0	4 - 0 - 0	UK, ME
Hammond R F*	RAAF	248	3+1ftl - 1 - 1½	3+1ftl - 1 - 1½	UK, ME
Hayley-Bell D*	RAF	604, 255, 68, 96, 125	2 - 0 - 2	2 - 1 - 2	UK
Atcherley D F W*	RAF	25	3? - 0 - 0	3? - 0 - 0	UK
Cobley P C *	RAF	272	2 - 0 - 6?	2 - 0 - 6?	ME
Hammond D H *	RNZAF	272	1+2sh - 1 - 1 +4sh	1+2sh - 1 - 1 +4sh	ME
Inniss A R deL*	RAF	248, 39	?+3sh - 0 - 0	?+3sh - 0 - 0	UK, ME

The leading RCAF night-fighter pilot was Sqn Ldr R C 'Moose' Fumerton who was the fourth top-scorer on Beaufighters.

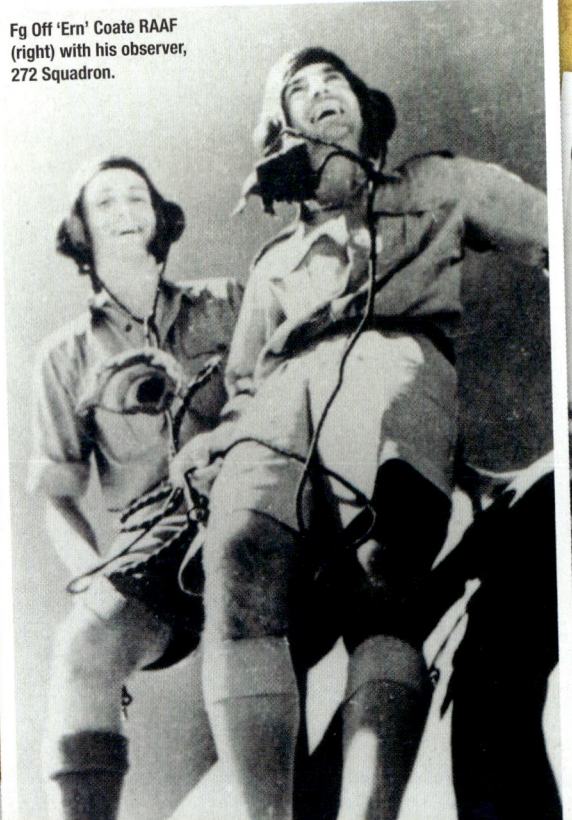

Fg Off 'Ern' Coate RAAF (right) with his observer, 272 Squadron.

Flt Sgt 'Maurice' Pring, 176 Squadron.

'Red' Modera resting in Kenya, 1945, after his time with 227 Squadron on Malta.

long-range fighter and strike roles, though these tasks would later merge to some extent. It again proved devastatingly effective against enemy bombers – and in supporting the campaign of the 8th Army in the desert – with many pilots building up large scores flying the type. When the USAAF arrived in North Africa and the Mediterranean, its night fighter squadrons also flew the Beaufighter with distinction.

Back home, the Beaufighter also pioneered the bomber support role – flying with the bomber streams to hunt out the enemy's own night-fighters; again with considerable success.

Further afield, Beaufighters also took on the Japanese, defending Indian ports against night bombers and sweeping on strike sorties all over Burma where it gained a fearsome reputation. Though the opportunities for air combat were few, several pilots became 'aces' in this theatre. It was the same over New Guinea and the Dutch East Indies, where RAAF squadrons, flying mainly in the strike role, took every opportunity to down enemy aircraft.

In total some 84 pilots became 'aces' flying Beaufighters while a further 39 achieved at least a part of their total on the type, though their names are not included here.

VISIT OUR ONLINE SHOP
TO VIEW OUR FULL RANGE OF SPECIAL MAGAZINES ABOUT **MILITARY AVIATION**

Key Shop

shop.keypublishing.com/specials

£8.99

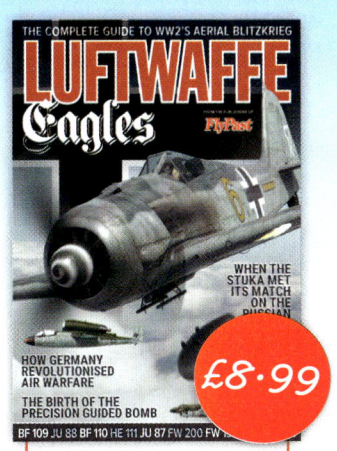

Originally published in 2014, this popular special examines the Luftwaffe of World War Two right from the invasion of Poland in September 1939. Prepared by the editorial team that brings you Britain's top-selling aviation monthly, FlyPast, this is a highly collectable tribute to a formidable air force.

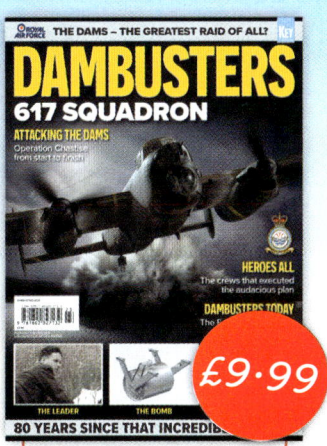

£9.99

On the 80th anniversary of the most famous Royal Air Force operation, Dambusters pays homage to the aircraft, crews and engineers who made the audacious 1943 raid possible. This 116-page special publication is a must-read for all enthusiasts of military aviation and World War II history.

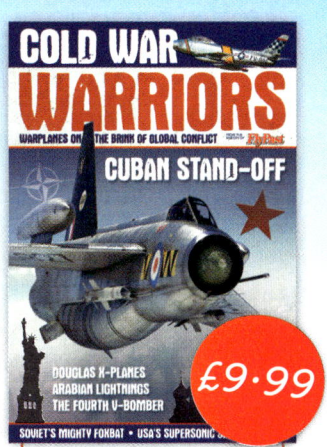

£9.99

As well as intercontinental ballistic missiles and high-tech warfare, the Cold War bore some of the most advanced and popular aircraft since World War Two. All of these are featured in this 100-page special from the team behind FlyPast magazine.

£8.99

The Wellington developed a reputation for being able to take a lot of punishment and still bring crews home. Reissued to commemorate 70 years since its retirement in 1953, this 100-page special from the team behind FlyPast magazine provides a much sought-after tribute to an incredible warplane.

£8.99

It was the period when Great Britain's aviation industry was established and grew to its zenith. Containing scores of period images, meticulously colourised, this new bookazine chronicles the wide variety of aircraft produced in Great Britain before 1950, portraying them in their full glory.

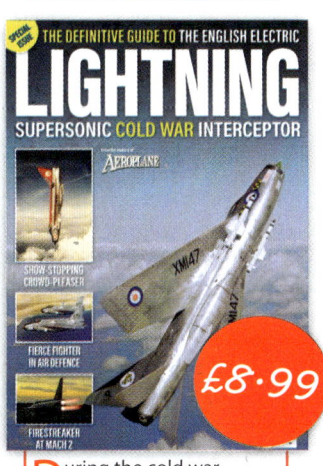

£8.99

During the cold war, the English Electric Lightning was the RAF's 'go to' interceptor fighter. Those that flew it loved it, those that faced it feared it. This 116-page special celebrates the history of the Lightning and charts its design, production, service, and the pilots that flew it.

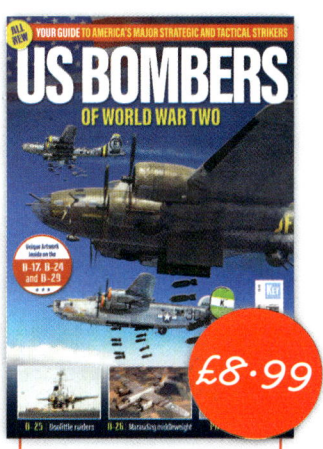

£8.99

The United States' bomber fleets undoubtedly made a huge contribution to the Allied victory in World War Two. This publication pays tribute to such aircraft as the B-25 Mitchell and B-26 Marauder that fought countless battles over deserts, jungles, and seas in pursuit of the ultimate victory that cost the lives of tens of thousands of aircrew.

£8.99

The de Havilland DH.98 Mosquito was one of the outstanding aircraft of World War Two, making a significant contribution to the Allied victory. It was also used for a succession of daring low level precision attacks against a range of targets, many of which are described in this 132-page special not seen for 10 years.

FREE P&P* when you order online at…
shop.keypublishing.com/specials

Call +44 (0)1780 480404 (Monday to Friday 9am-5.30pm GMT)

Also available from **W.H Smith** and all leading newsagents. Or download from **Pocketmags.com** or your native app store - search *Aviation Specials*

SUBSCRIBERS don't forget to use your **£2 OFF DISCOUNT CODE!**

*Free 2nd class P&P on all UK & BFPO orders. Overseas charges apply.

ADAPT, IMPROVE, EXCEL

SOME OF THE GREATEST WARPLANES STARTED LIFE AS STOP-GAPS. M L WYNCH DESCRIBES THE EVOLUTION OF THE BEAUFIGHTER

"...AN APPRECIATIVE AIR MINISTRY ORDERED 150 TYPE 142MS OFF THE FILTON DRAWING BOARDS. THE INCREDIBLE BLENHEIM HAD BEEN CONCEIVED."

There are times when the luxury of a blank sheet of paper on a designer's drawing board is not an option. Time constraints require a more practical solution. Some of the best aircraft of World War Two were adaptations of another type, very likely one that was not overly graced with achievement. Despite such make-do-and-mend origins, these machines excelled - such was the Beaufighter.

Bristol's big, capable, formidably-armed fighter was the third of a dynasty of twin-engined warriors and all of them owed their lineage to a newspaper mogul. More members of the family followed but it was the Blenheim and the Beaufighter that took the lion's share of the accolades.

In the early 1930s, the Bristol Aeroplane Company was best known for fighters and a lot of hopeful prototypes. From 1933

Above: Australian-built Beaufort VIIIs of 100 Squadron RAAF. From the Beaufort came the 'quick-fix' Beaufighter. Key-Gordon Swanborough collection

Captain Frank Barnwell's design office at Filton was engaged on what would become the Bombay bomber-transport and this provided much experience of monoplanes and larger structures. On June 23, 1935, the prototype Bombay first flew and started to occupy the production shops. But there was not much to keep the slide-rules and draughting pens busy, so the designers turned to pastures new.

One of the 'what-ifs' they came up

'Britain First', the Bristol 142 executive transport that gave rise to all of Bristol's wartime twin-engined warplanes. Bristol

The Type 142M, the first Blenheim. Bristol

The Beaufort prototype, L4441, first flown on October 15, 1938.

with was a very clean-looking eight-seater twin-engined retractable that might appeal to businesses and the rich - a 1930s Learjet. Lord Rothermere, patron of the *Daily Mail* and a great supporter of British aviation, got wind of the project and expressed an interest. This was less about acquiring a high-speed corporate transport, and more about putting a shot-in-the-arm of the industry to enable it to show what it could achieve when released from the fetters of officialdom.

In March 1934 Rothermere ordered a single Type 142, which he declared would carry the name *Britain First*. Bristol informed the Air Ministry of the purchase and there were no objections. It was a golden opportunity; private enterprise paying for the development of what could be the next generation of warplane.

The Type 142 had its maiden flight on April 12, 1935, and was followed on January 20, 1936, by the bigger Type 143. When *Britain First* was evaluated at the Aeroplane &

BRISTOL TWINS DYNASTY

Apr 12, 1935	Type 142, *Britain First*, first flown	
Jan 20, 1936	Type 143, an enlarged eight-passenger version, first flown	
Jun 25, 1936	Type 142M Blenheim I first flown	
Sep 24, 1937	Type 149 Bolingbroke I first flown. Type renamed the Blenheim IV, although the name Bolingbroke was kept for Canadian production	
Oct 15, 1938	Type 152 Beaufort I first flown	
Jul 17, 1939	Type 156 Beaufighter I first flown	
Feb 24, 1941	Type 160 Bisley I first flown. Type renamed Blenheim V	
Feb 4, 1943	Type 163 Buckingham I, medium day/night bomber, first flown	
Oct 27, 1944	Type 166 Buckmaster I crew trainer first flown. RAF Beaufighters retired from frontline use during 1944	
Dec 4, 1944	Type 164 Brigand TF.I torpedo fighter first flown	
Sep 1945	Last Beaufighter comes off production line, TF.X SR919	
1946	RAAF Beauforts and RCAF Bolingbrokes retired	
1956	Last Blenheims retired from flying in Finland	
1958	Last Brigands and Buckmasters retired from RAF service	
May 12, 1960	Last fight of a RAF Beaufighter, TT.10 RD761	

The second prototype, R2057, with dihedral on the tailplane.

Below: **The first Beaufighter, R2052.**

Armament Experimental Establishment (A&AEE) at Martlesham Heath in Suffolk it ruffled feathers. Here was a twin with obvious potential to become a 'heavy' fighter or a bomber that had a top speed 54mph (87km/h) *faster* that the state-of-the-art Gloster Gladiator biplane fighter that had just been ordered for the RAF.

Point made, Lord Rothermere presented *Britain First* to the nation. In August 1935 an appreciative Air Ministry ordered 150 military-configured Type 142Ms off the Filton drawing boards. The incredible Blenheim had been conceived.

BATTLES, CASTLES AND DUKES

On June 25, 1936 the prototype Blenheim I flew, and up to 1945 over 6,000 had been built in the UK, Canada and Finland serving in all theatres in a galaxy of roles in a variety of models. This is a story all of its own and need concern us only because *Britain First* provided the airframe that formed the basis of the Beaufighter.

It was clear that Frank Barnwell's Blenheim had huge development

NEXT GENERATION BUCKINGHAM

A larger version of the Beaufort and Beaufighter, a medium bomber was schemed as the Type 162 Beaumont. This was superseded by the Type 163 aiming at Specification 7/41. This was given the name Buckingham, perhaps to maintain the 'palace' theme. With a four-man crew. Changes to the requirement, and the success of the Beaufighter, delayed the first flight of the prototype (DX249, illustrated) until February 4, 1943. At one point, it was re-thought as a torpedo-bomber to replace the Beaufighter; this project was given the name Buccaneer. After the four prototypes, production was terminated at 65 units, most destined straight for storage and the scrapyard. Some were converted to C.1 transports with seating for four passengers.

Above: **A Mk.VI carrying a torpedo and without the inner starboard undercarriage door. This view also shows the asymmetric layout of the wing machine-guns – note the two cartridge ejection slots in the port wing (near the landing light) and four in the starboard wing.** Key Collection

Above, left: **Possibly second prototype, R2057, showing the Fairey-Youngman bellows-type air brakes.** Peter Green collection

potential and the Bolingbroke and Bisley represented how the Type 142M airframe evolved (see the *Bristol Twins Dynasty* panel). A major re-think of the format came with the Type 152, ultimately to meet Specification 10/36 for a twin-engined, four-crew, anti-shipping aircraft capable of carrying two torpedoes or bombs, plus defensive armament.

In keeping with the 'stately' naming of the Blenheim, the new bomber was given the name Beaufort, with the consent of the 10th Duke of Beaufort. In the 14th century, the family purloined a castle of the same name in the Champagne region of France.

While we're at it, the Blenheim took its name from a misspelling of the Battle of Blindheim in Bavaria in which the Duke of Marlborough and Prince Eugene of Savoy thrashed the Franco-Bavarian forces of Louis XIV on August 13, 1704. Marlborough celebrated with the creation of the Versailles-esque Blenheim Palace near Woodstock in Oxfordshire - perhaps Bristol's incredibly versatile twin was named after the palace and not the battle.

RE-THINKING THE BLENHEIM

It is simplistic to see the Beaufort as a 'Blenheim with bits on'. Unlike the Bolingbroke and the Bisley, the Beaufort was a re-think of the Blenheim's format and took account of lessons learned during the development of its illustrious forebear. The Blenheim largely employed 'plate-and-angle' construction; the Beaufort used light alloy forgings and extrusions.

Dimensionally, there was little difference: span 56ft 4in (17.16m) against the Blenheim IV's 57ft 10in and length 42ft 9in and 44ft 3in, respectively. This was due to the lengthened nose section, the widened (and deepened) fuselage to take a crew of four, a turret and a weapons bay. Wing area increased from 469ft^2 (43.5m^2) to 503ft^2. But it is the weights that show the leap taken by the new machine: the Blenheim IV was 9,800lb (4,445kg) unladen and 14,400lb loaded, while the Beaufort was 13,100lb and 21,230lb respectively.

The prototype Beaufort, L4441, took to the air for the first time on October 15, 1938, powered by Bristol Taurus IIIs. At Thorney Island on the Hampshire coast, 22 Squadron put the new type into service in January 1940. From 1939, Australia built the Beaufort as well, opting for Pratt & Whitney Twin Wasps. Beauforts served with distinction in Europe, the Middle East, the Far East and the Pacific but, as is the case with the Blenheim, this is not the place for a major history of its exploits. In the UK 1,429 were built, while in Australia another 700 were produced.

When L4441 got airborne at Filton on its inaugural flight, there was someone missing in the gathering of onlookers. On August 2, 1938 Frank Barnwell died while piloting a single-seat ultra-light of his own design: the Barnwell BSW Mk.I G-AFID, powered by a 28hp (20.8kW) Scott two-cylinder. Frank was making the little machine's second flight when it plunged to the ground. The world had been robbed of a great talent.

With a heavy heart, Leslie George 'LG' Frise, assistant chief designer since 1915, took over from his late friend, colleague and mentor. The combination of Barnwell and Frise had been instrumental in the success of the Bristol company. Thanks to 'LG's guidance the Filton design office was able to continue seamlessly. While Frank and 'LG' had shared the gestation of the Beaufort, the Beaufighter as a concept and final product was down to Frise.

INSPIRED 'SPORTS MODEL'

Barnwell and Frise had been examining the possibilities of a four-cannon fighter - this would offer exceptional 'punch'. Westland has secured a contract for W E W Petter's revolutionary single-seat twin Rolls-Royce Peregrine-powered fighter, with four 20mm cannon in the nose. The prototype, the Whirlwind I, first flew on October 11, 1938, four days before the maiden flight of the Beaufort. The Whirlwind was to prove a disappointment, but the concept of concentrated fire from guns clustered in the forward fuselage remained a potent one.

Even in 1938, it was clear that while the Blenheim *might* be able to carry cannon, a major leap in performance was required. Fighter Command needed a two-seat 'heavy' fighter for day and night interceptions. In the weeks following the Beaufort's debut, 'LG' came up with an inspired adaption of its airframe.

Retaining the wings, centre section, tail unit and undercarriage, a new slimline fuselage with a pilot and observer in tandem and a weapons bay below the centre section carrying four 20mm cannon was added. Gone were the 1,065hp Taurus radials, and in their place was a pair of 1,670hp Bristol Hercules.

A lot of thought had gone into making the Beaufort far easier to mass produce than the Blenheim. Frise continued this mind-set. The new machine could be built mostly using the existing jigs. 'LG' was offering the ability to 'mix and match' on the production line.

With encouragement from the Air Ministry, in January 1939 'LG' revealed sketches of a 'family' based on the 'platform' of the Beaufort. The Type 156

Top: Beaufighter IIf R2402 of 255 Squadron, based at Coltishall, late 1941. Pete West © 2012

Above: For a while in 1941, production of airframes outstripped the supply of engines. Fuselage sections stacked at Old Mixon. Peter Green collection

NEXT GENERATION: BUCKMASTER

The Buckingham may have been outdated almost before it entered service, but the airframe was considered ideal to become an advanced crew trainer. The first of two Type 166 Buckmaster T.Is (TJ714, illustrated) had its maiden flight on October 27, 1944. It was followed by 110 production examples.

Above: Undercarriage retraction tests, probably at the Old Mixon factory. Peter Green collection

was his initial thinking, as described above. The Type 157 was a three-crew bomber with a power-operated turret; effectively a non-torpedo capable Beaufort replacement. The Type 158 was a more comprehensive fighter version and the Filton design office called this the 'Sports Model'. The 156 was to be expedited and in March it was given a name that reflected the thinking behind it: the Beaufort-Fighter, or Beaufighter.

RAPID DEPLOYMENT

Just over six months after the initial layouts had been presented, Capt Cyril 'Cy' F Unwins took the Beaufighter prototype, R2052, into the air for the first time on July 17, 1939, at Filton. This was an astoundingly swift achievement. In the same month, Specification F17/39 was drawn up covering the production of 300 Hercules-powered Beaufighter Is.

As 'insurance' against production/performance problems with the Hercules, the Rolls-Royce Griffon was proposed, with as few changes to the airframe as possible. This was a tall order; fitting a 12-cylinder 60-degree 'vee' format in-line, 30in (76cm) wide and 46in tall, into the same bulkhead and fairing as a 14-cylinder two-row radial of 55in diameter, would take some doing.

Tests showed that R2052 had a maximum speed of 335mph at 17,000ft - the Hawker Hurricane I was capable of 316mph. But evaluation of the fully-fitted R2054 with Hercules IIIs at the A&AEE, by then at Boscombe Down, near Salisbury, during June 1940, had brought this down to 309mph.

So development of the Type 158 continued under the designation

NEXT GENERATION: BRIGAND

Just as the Beaufighter came about as a slimmed-down fighter fuselage on a Beaufort fuselage, so the Type 164 Brigand was developed in a similar manner from the Buckingham/Buckmaster format. The Brigand was conceived as a replacement for the Beaufighter as a torpedo-fighter, the TF.I. The first of four prototypes, MX988 flew on December 4, 1944 (second example, MX991, illustrated).

As development proceeded, it was clear that this type of warplane was out-moded and only a few TF.Is were completed before production standardised on the B.1 which entered RAF service in 1949 as a light bomber. Additionally Brigands served in the weather reconnaissance role as the Met.3 and the T.4 and T.5 crew trainers. In all 147 were built, with three supplied to Pakistan.

Below: Conversion work under way at Hucknall on Mk.II T3177 to become the Griffon IIB test-bed.

Rear aspect of a Mk.IIf (above) and a TT.10.

Beaufighter III; Griffon versions would be Mk.IVs. But by this point, the Battle of Britain was raging and trials of the Beaufighter with airborne interception (AI) radar showed a formidable night-fighter that could be deployed with rapidity. The RAF quickly realised that although the Type 158 offered great promise, with the 156 it already had a 'Sports Model'.

Beaufighter TF.X NE255 of 404 Squadron RCAF, Davidstow Moor, 1944.
Pete West © 2012

The production line at Filton was at full tilt and plans were made to sub-contract. Bristol managed a huge Ministry of Aircraft Production plant at Old Mixon, near Weston-super-Mare and this was to eventually take over from Filton. Fairey Aviation at Stockport, near Manchester, and Rootes Securities at Blythe Bridge in Staffordshire, also ran MAP factories building Beaufighters. The 100th 'Beau' was ready for service on December 7, 1940 and in November 1942 the 1,000th appeared - an exceptional achievement. (See the panels for production details.)

The first operational Beaufighter unit was 25 Squadron at Debden in Essex, receiving examples in September. The inaugural Coastal Command unit was 252 at Chivenor, Devon, in December 1940. Mk.Is configured for Fighter Command were referred to as Mk.Ifs, while those bound for Coastal Command were Mk.Ics. (See the *Squadron Directory* for full details of units and *Deserts and Seas,* which deals

MAN BEHIND THE BEAUFIGHTER

Gaining a Bachelor of Science degree at Bristol University, Leslie George Frise signed up as a Sub Lieutenant in the Royal Naval Air Service in 1915. This was short-lived; his engineering abilities had been drawn to the attention of Frank Barnwell and 'LG' (as he was known) was offered the post of Assistant Chief Designer with Bristol. The pair became a formidable force, good friends and vital to the success of the Filton-based company.

'LG' started off with stress calculations and drawings for what became the F.2b Fighter. In 1919 he was instrumental in designing and setting up a wind tunnel; a novelty with most aircraft companies at that time. Always looking at ways to improve the controllability of aircraft, he invented the slotted aileron, which was patented in 1921. It was employed worldwide and became known universally as the Frise Aileron. In the 1920s the combination of Barnwell and Frise pioneers the strip-steel construction method, contributing greatly to the dominance of the Bulldog fighter in RAF orders.

Peter Green collection

The death of Frank Barnwell came as a severe blow to 'LG' and everybody at Bristol. Promoted to chief designer, 'LG' masterminded the Beaufighter and went on to design the Buckingham and others in the 'twin' family. As the war came to an end, he had carried out much of the work on the massive Brabazon airliner and created the Bristol 170 civilian freighter and helped to establish the helicopter division.

By early 1946 the never-ending demands of the war years caught up with 'LG' and he resigned due to ill-health. He took up the post of Technical Director and Chief Engineer with Percival Aircraft (part of the Hunting Group) working on the Provost, Jet Provost, the Pembroke series and the abortive P.74 before retiring. He died in 1979.

Frontal aspect of the Beaufighter If (top) and Mk.IIf.

with 252 Squadron.)

At Ford in Sussex, the Fighter Interception Unit initially tried out AI Mk.IV in the Beaufighter. This worked well and it became standard on night-prowling 'Beaus'. These were readily identifiable by the 'arrowhead' aerials on the nose and leading edges of the wing. With the advent of the Beaufighter VI (see below) in 1942, AI Mk.IV was introduced, but gave way to the centimetric Mk.VII contained in a distinctive 'thimble' radome on the nose. Later, AI Mk.VIII took over and this was also used for the Beaufighter X (of which more soon). The Mk.VIII could be 'tweaked' for use as an anti-surface vessel radar giving Coastal Command aircraft the ability hunt as well as strike.

With potent engines coupled to a comparatively short fuselage, the Beaufighter suffered from longitudinal stability. To counter this, Mk.I R2268 was fitted with twin fins and rudders, but it was found that there was an easier 'fix'. Mk.Is R2057 and R2270 had their tailplane and elevators given a 12-degree dihedral and this improved things dramatically, being incorporated on all but night-fighters.

Fighter Command wanted an effective dive brake to allow for well-governed deceleration when homing in on an enemy in the black void. Fitted with Fairey-Youngman bellows-operated brakes at the mid-wing trailing edge, R2057 proved the system's worth. Fighter Command did not take up the mod, but Coastal Command realised its potential for maritime strike.

MERLINS
AND GRIFFONS

As there were some development problems with the Hercules, particularly the Mk.VI, and pressing demands for that variant for the Short Stirling III bomber, another powerplant was deemed prudent to ensure Beaufighter production. As related above, the Rolls-Royce Griffon was put forward for the projected Mk.IV. But in the summer

Beaufighter Mk.10 cockpit.
Peter Green collection

Mk.If R2268 was used to try out twin fins and rudders to improve longitudinal stability.
Key-Gordon Swanborough collection

of 1940, the Fleet Air Arm had approved development of the Fairey Firefly carrier-borne fighter. Those plans looked set to swallow up every available Griffon IIB, although the prototype Firefly did not get airborne until December 22, 1941.

In place of the Griffon, the Merlin XX was substituted, although this was also much in demand. Avro was working on the re-engined Manchester, and the Merlin-powered Lancaster was also destined for Merlin XXs. (The first 'Lanc' took to the air on January 9, 1941.) Based upon the outboard powerplants of the forthcoming Lancaster, Rolls-Royce developed a 'fix' that coupled Merlin XXs with the Beaufighter I airframe and Morris Motors at Cowley undertook production of a self-contained, pre-plumbed and wired engine, cowling and mounting.

The first Beaufighter II (as the Merlin version was designated) took to the air with an interim Merlin X at Hucknall, Notts, in July 1940. As with the radial-engined Beaufighter, longitudinal stability was a problem and Mk.IIf T3032 was given an enlarged fin and rudder and eventually a dorsal fin extending aft from just behind the observer's 'blister'. The Mk.II became a dedicated night-fighter and 600 Squadron at Colerne, Wiltshire, was first to adopt it in April 1941.

Mk.IIs R2274 and R2306 were used for trials with a four-gun power-operated turret fitted just behind the cockpit. Designated the Mk.V, it was not taken any further. Rolls-Royce used a pair of Mk.IIs for high-altitude trials of Merlin 61s and T3177 as a test-bed for the Firefly's Griffon IIB. (For more details of powerplants and armament, take a look at the *Power and Punch* sections, respectively.)

'SIXES' AND 'TENS'

Rated at 1,615hp, the Hercules VI entered mass production in 1942 and powered Lancaster IIs, Handley Page Halifax IIIs and VIIs, Short Stirling IIIs, IVs and Vs and Vickers Wellington XIs and XIIs. This remarkable engine provided the next leap in the Beaufighter's evolution. Coincidentally, the fitting of the Hercules VI created the Beaufighter VI. These machines began to replace Beauforts in the coastal strike role by May 1942.

By late 1941

Weston-super-Mare-built TF.X RD758 with under wing weapon racks, a 200-gallon ferry tank, dihedral tailplane and large fin fillet. The lettering 'SNAKE' denotes that it is destined for Air Command South East Asia and is not to be diverted to other theatres during the long ferry flight. It did not enter service in SEAC, instead coming back to Filton for conversion to TT.10 target-tug. KEC

Mk.IIf T3032 experimented with several tail shapes, including a very tall fin and rudder.

BEAUFIGHTER IF

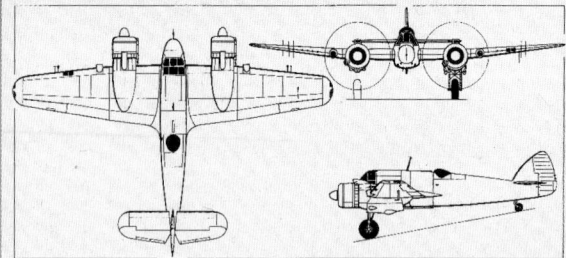

© KEY 2012

Powerplant	Two 1,400hp (1,044kW) Bristol Hercules III, X or XI
Dimensions	Span 57ft 0in (17.37m) Length 41ft 4in (12.59m) Height 15ft 10in (4.82m) Wing area 503ft² (46.72m²)
Weights	Empty 13,800lb (6,259kg) All-up 21,000lb (9,526kg)
Performance	Max speed 330mph (531km/h) Service ceiling 29,000ft (8,839m)
Serial ranges	Prototypes: R2052 to R2060; Mk.If R2063 to R2269, T4623 to T4647, V8219 to V8385, X7540 to X7879; Mk.Ic T3228 to T3355, T4648 to T5099
Built by	Bristol at Filton and Old Mixon, Weston-super-Mare; Fairey at Stockport. Total production of Mk.Is (including prototypes): 915

BEAUFIGHTER II

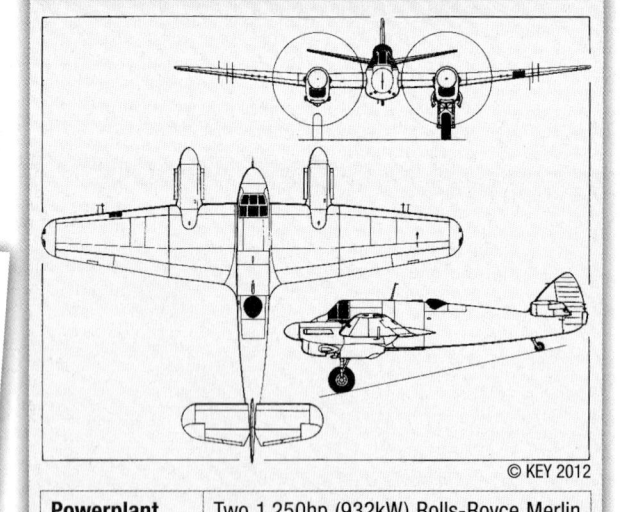

© KEY 2012

Powerplant	Two 1,250hp (932kW) Rolls-Royce Merlin XX
Dimensions	Span 57ft 0in (17.37m) Length 42ft 9in (13.0m) Height 15ft 10in (4.82m) Wing area 503ft² (46.72m²)
Weights	Empty 13,800lb (6,259kg) All-up 21,000lb (9,526kg)
Performance	Max speed 330mph (531km/h) Service ceiling 29,000ft (8,839m)
Serial ranges	Prototypes R2058, R2061, R2062; R2270 to R2479, T3009 to T3447, V8131 to V8218
Built by	Bristol at Filton. Total Mk.II production (including prototypes): 450

BEAUFIGHTER TF.X

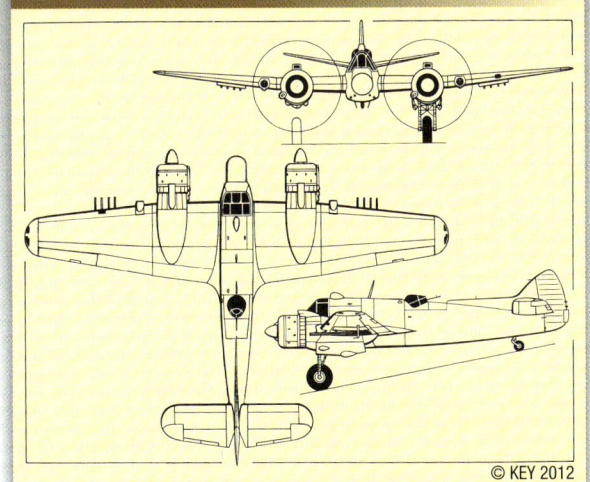

Possibly the second prototype R2057 showing the Fairey-Youngman bellows-type air brakes. Peter Green collection

Powerplant	Two 1,735hp (1,294kW) Bristol Hercules XVIII
Dimensions	Span 57ft 0in (17.37m) Length 42ft 6in (12.95m) Height 15ft 10in (4.82m) Wing area 503ft^2 (46.72m^2)
Weights	Empty 15,600lb (7,076kg) All-up 25,400lb (11,521kg)
Performance	Max speed 330mph (531km/h) Service ceiling 29,000ft (8,839m)
Serial ranges	Mk.VI V8386 to V8901, X7880 to X8269, BT286 to BT303, EL145 to EL218, KV896 to KV981, KW101 to KW203, MM838 to MM948, ND139 to ND322. Mk.VIc T5100 to T352, X7925 to X8099, EL219 to EL534, JL421 to JL875. Mk.X JM268 to JM417, KW277 to KW416, LX779 to LX799, LZ113 to LZ544, NE193 to NE832, NT888 to NT999, NV113 to NV632, RD130 to RD867, SR910 to SR919. Mk.XI JL876 to JL948, JM105 to JM267
Built by	Bristol at Filton and Old Mixon, West-on-super-Mare, Rootes Securities at Blythe Bridge, Staffs. Total production: Mk.VIs 1,831; Mk.X 2,205; Mk.XI 163

the Beaufort was in need of replacement as a torpedo carrier and there was a proposal to harness the Beaufighter's wings, powerplant and tail with the fuselage of its predecessor. 'LG' and his team thought that this was a retrograde step. The proposal from Bristol was to forget the ability to stow torpedoes internally and to sling one under a 'Beau' with minimal alterations.

Below: First operational unit to fly the Beaufighter was 25 Squadron in September 1940 and many photo-opportunities were staged between sorties. KEC

This was approved on April 13, 1942, and Bristol again showed how quickly it could react. Twelve days later, Mk.VI X8065 was ready for inspection and on May 8, 1942, it was ferried to the Torpedo Development Unit at Gosport in Hampshire for intensive trials. Tragically, TDU's 'boss' Wg Cdr Shaw was killed when an engine failed and X8065 spiralled into the ground on June 16. By then plaudits for the Beaufighter VI torpedo-fighter had assured the type's future. In August 254 Squadron at North Coates on the Lincolnshire coast started training and its first strikes were made off the Norwegian coast before the year was out. The 'TorBeau' had been born.

As might be assumed from the list of types given above, the Hercules VI was optimised for high altitudes. The thin air of 20,000ft or so was not where Coastal Command did its business. Demand for torpedo-toting Beaufighters was such that an initial batch was produced with Hercules VIs or XVIs and these were designated Beaufighter VI (ITF) - for interim torpedo-fighter). The definitive answer was the Hercules XVII and with this engine and torpedo shackles the Beaufighter TF.X came into being. Non-torpedo versions were Mk.XIs.

The Beaufighter XII was not proceeded with, although its beefed-up wing was used in the final batches of TF.Xs.

With radar and a torpedo, fuel for a long patrol, a Mk.X was a heavily-laden beast of burden on take-off - as much as 25,400lb. (That's 400lb *more* than *two* fully-loaded Blenheim Is!) An engine out at this point would very likely be lethal, but any sort of swing that developed could have the same tragic results. The Merlin-engined Mk.II had suffered from similar issues and enlarged elevators and a dorsal fin as tested on that variant helped to provide greater control response. The first Mk.Xs entered service with 248 Squadron at Predannack in Cornwall in June 1943.

The story of Australian Beaufighters is given in the chapter *Whispering Death*. Post-war the type enjoyed limited success overseas as outlined in *Under Other Flags*. Production in the UK came to a halt in September 1945, with TF.X SR919 at Weston-super-Mare taking the accolade as the last of the breed. That machine and others saw extended life with the last Beaufighter variant, the TT.10. For the swansong of the Beaufighter in RAF service, turn to the chapter *Tugging at Sleeves*.

POWE

"TWO ENGINES HOTLY PURSUED BY AN AIRFRAME" WAS A TONGUE-IN-CHEEK DESCRIPTION OF THE INCREASINGLY POTENT BEAUFIGHTER THE FOUR POWERPLANTS THAT DROVE THE MIGHTY 'BEAU' ARE DETAILED HERE

BRISTOL HERCULES

Above from left: **The exhaust arrangement of the Hercules and a detailed view of the cowlings; An enlarged supercharger intake above the cowling on an anonymous Beaufighter. To the right is the leading edge-mounted oil cooler; Detail view of a Beaufighter I's port engine, with the rear 'gills' open and the propeller spinner removed; Detail of the cylinder heads on a Beaufighter I.**

The Hercules was the most popular, and adaptive, Beaufighter powerplant.

Type:	14-cylinder, two-row, sleeve-valve, air-cooled radial
Beaufighter prototype	Hercules II of 1,375hp (1,025hp) fitted to R2055
Beaufighter I:	Hercules III, X or XI of 1,400hp (1,044kW)
Beaufighter III:	Hercules VI with reverse-flow cooling - not proceeded with
Beaufighter VI:	Hercules VI, VII/Hercules 26 or XVI of 1,600hp (1,193kW)
Beaufighter VII:	Hercules 26 with Bendix carburettors for Australia - not proceeded with
Beaufighter X or XI:	Hercules XVII of 1,735hp (1,294kW)
Beaufighter XII:	Hercules 27 - not proceeded with
Beaufighter Mk.21	Hercules XVIII of 1,735hp (1,294kW)
Other applications:	Armstrong Whitworth Albemarle, Avro Lancaster II, Avro York II, Handley Page Halifax III, VII, Saro Lerwick, Short Stirling, Vickers Wellington
Notes:	The Hercules XI ran on 100 Octane fuel (introduced in 1940, replacing 87 Octane) and replaced the Hercules III. A Beaufighter VIc flew as a test-bed for the 1,600hp (1,193kW) Hercules 130 in 1946 for the Handley Page Hermes II and Vickers Viking airliners.

Main image: **The prototype Beaufighter R2052 at Filton in the summer of 1939, fitted with Hercules ISMs and de Havilland propellers.** Bristol

Left: **Superb detail of a Merlin XX-powered Mk.II.**

Right: A Mk.VI with a Hercules VI with a circular, tapered assembly cowling; testing for the Buckingham.

Far right: What is assumed to be a ground-running 'slave' four-bladed propeller.

Bottom right: Trial shrouds for the exhausts on a Merlin XX-powered Mk.II.

ROLLS-ROYCE MERLIN

Ground runs, with some panels removed, of Mk.II prototype R2058.
Key-Gordon Swanborough collection

Type:	12-cylinder, two-speed, single-stage supercharged 'vee' format
Beaufighter prototype	Merlin X of 1,145hp (854kW) fitted to R2058
Beaufighter II or V:	Merlin XX of 1,250hp (932kW)
Other applications:	Avro Lancaster, Boulton Paul Defiant, Handley Page Halifax II, Hawker Hurricane II, Supermarine Spitfire III
Notes:	Two of the Beaufighter II prototypes became test-beds for the Merlin 61 of 1,280hp (954kW)

ROLLS-ROYCE GRIFFON

The Griffon Beaufighter, T3177, with four-bladed propellers, 'arrowhead' radar on the nose. Key-Gordon Swanborough collection

Type:	12-cylinder, two-speed, single-stage supercharged 'vee' format
Beaufighter II:	Griffon IIB of 1,720hp (1,283kW) on test-bed T3177
Other applications:	Fairey Firefly I, Hawker Henley, Hawker Tempest III, Supermarine Spitfire IV and XX
Notes:	Early in the gestation of the Beaufighter, the Griffon was considered as the alternative powerplant to the Hercules. The Beaufighter IV would have been Griffon-powered. Demands elsewhere meant that the Griffon was not chosen for the 'Beau' and the Merlin was substituted

Far left: **A view of an experimental exhaust shroud on a Mk.II, with the leading edge at the top left.**

Left: **Exhaust trials with a Mk.II.**

All Peter Green collection unless noted

WRIGHT DOUBLE CYCLONE

Fairey-built Mk.Ic A19-2 re-engined in Australia with Double Cyclones - note the significantly enlarged nacelles. Key-Gordon Swanborough collection

Type:	14-cylinder, two-row, air-cooled radial
Beaufighter Ic:	Wright Double Cyclone GR-2600-A5B of 1,600hp (1,193kW) with enlarged nacelles fitted to A19-2
Other applications:	(R-2600) including Curtiss SB2C Helldiver, Douglas A-20 Havoc, Grumman TBM Avenger, North American B-25 Mitchell, Vultee A-35 Vengeance
Note:	Double Cyclone chosen as powerplant for Australian Beaufighters, as the Mks VIII and IX, if production of the Hercules XVIII stalled

BEAUFIGHTER SQUADRON DIRECTORY

ANDREW THOMAS CHRONICLES THE UNITS THAT FLEW THE 'BEAU'

ROYAL AIR FORCE

Note: # - partial equipment only

5 SQUADRON
- **Badge:** A maple leaf
- **Motto:** Frangas non flectes (Thou mayst break but shall not break me)
- **Variant/s:** TT.10#
- **Dates:** Jan 1950 to Sep 1951
- **Role:** TT
- **Theatre(s):** UK

17 SQUADRON
- **Badge:** A gauntlet
- **Motto:** Excellere contende (Strive to excel)
- **Variant/s:** TT.10#
- **Dates:** May 1949 to Mar 1951
- **Role:** TT
- **Theatre(s):** UK

20 SQUADRON
- **Badge:** In front of a rising sun, an eagle perched on a sword
- **Motto:** Facta non verba (Deeds not words)
- **Variant/s:** TT.10#
- **Dates:** Feb 1949 to Oct 1951
- **Role:** TT
- **Theatre(s):** UK

22 SQUADRON
- **Badge:** On a torteau, a Maltese cross with 'pi' superimposed
- **Motto:** Preux et audacieux (Valiant and brave)
- **Variant/s:** X
- **Dates:** Jun 1944 to Sep 1945
- **Role:** TCS
- **Theatre(s):** FE

Beaufighter TF.X NE478 of 22 Squadron, 1944.

25 SQUADRON
- **Badge:** A hawk on a gauntlet
- **Motto:** Ferines tego (Striking I defend)
- **Variant/s:** If
- **Dates:** Oct 1940 to Jan 1943
- **Role:** NF
- **Theatre(s):** UK

27 SQUADRON
- **Badge:** An elephant
- **Motto:** Quam celerrime ad astra (All speed to the stars)
- **Variant/s:** VI, X
- **Dates:** Nov 1942 to Feb 1946
- **Role:** GA
- **Theatre(s):** FE

29 SQUADRON
- **Badge:** An eagle preying on a buzzard
- **Motto:** Impiger et acer (Energetic and keen)
- **Variant/s:** If, VIf
- **Dates:** Nov 1940 to May 1943
- **Role:** NF
- **Theatre(s):** UK

34 SQUADRON
- **Badge:** In front of a crescent moon, a wolf
- **Motto:** Lupus vult, lupus volat (Wolf wishes, wolf flies)
- **Variant/s:** TT.10#
- **Dates:** Feb 1949 to Jul 1951
- **Role:** TT
- **Theatre(s):** UK

39 SQUADRON
- **Badge:** A winged bomb
- **Motto:** Die noctuque (By day and by night)
- **Variant/s:** X
- **Dates:** Jul 1943 to Feb 1945
- **Role:** TCS
- **Theatre(s):** MedME

42 SQUADRON
- **Badge:** On a globe, a figure of Perseus
- **Motto:** Fortiter in re (Bravely in action)
- **Variant/s:** TF.X
- **Dates:** Oct 1946 to Oct 1947
- **Role:** TCS
- **Theatre(s):** UK

45 SQUADRON
- **Badge:** A winged camel
- **Motto:** Per ardua surgo (Through difficulties I arise)
- **Variant/s:** TF.10
- **Dates:** Dec 1945 to Feb 1950
- **Role:** GA
- **Theatre(s):** FE

46 SQUADRON
- **Badge:** Three arrowheads
- **Motto:** We rise to conquer
- **Variant/s:** If, VIf, X#
- **Dates:** May 1942 to Dec 1944
- **Role:** NF
- **Theatre(s):** MedME

47 SQUADRON
- **Badge:** In front of a fountain, a demoiselle crane's head
- **Motto:** Nili nomen roboris omen (The name of the Nile is an omen of our strength)
- **Variant/s:** X
- **Dates:** Jun 1943 to Oct 1944, Dec 1944 to Apr 1945
- **Role:** TCS, GA
- **Theatre(s):** MedME, FE

68 SQUADRON
- **Badge:** A tawny owl's head
- **Motto:** Vzdy pripraven (Always ready)
- **Variant/s:** If, VIf
- **Dates:** May 41-Jul 44
- **Role:** NF
- **Theatre(s):** UK

69 SQUADRON
- **Badge:** In front of an anchor, a telescope
- **Motto:** With vigilance we serve
- **Variant/s:** Ic#
- **Dates:** Jan 1941 to Feb 1944
- **Role:** PR
- **Theatre(s):** MedME

84 SQUADRON
- **Badge:** A scorpion

Right: **A TF.X of 18 Squadron SAAF unleashing rocket projectiles on a German Barracks in Yugoslavia, 1945.**

Left: **Mk.If V8324 'Bambi' of 29 Squadron, late 1942.**

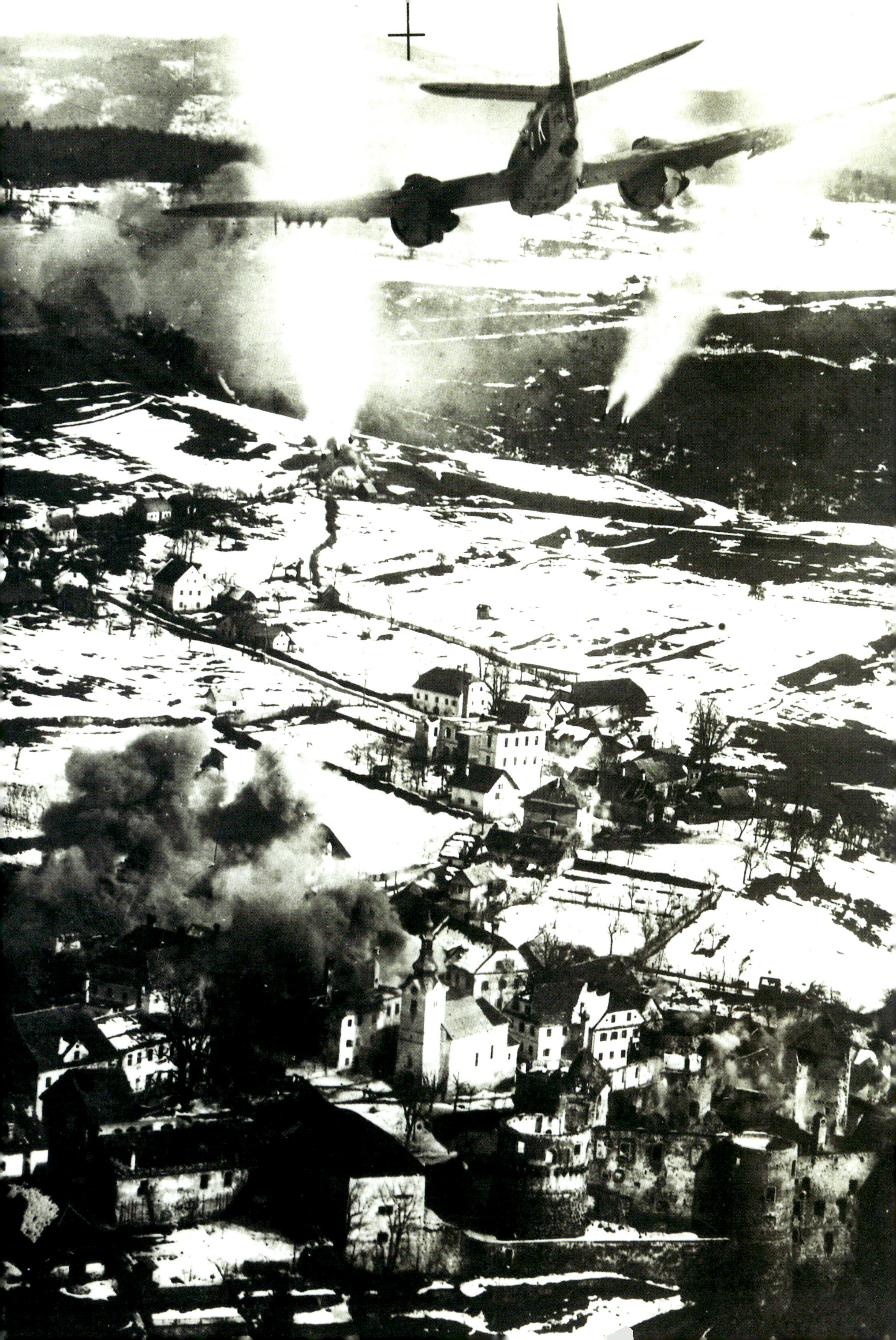

Motto: Scorpiones pungent (Scorpions sting)
Variant/s: TF.10
Dates: Nov 1946 to Mar 1949
Role: GA
Theatre(s): FE, MedME

89 SQUADRON
Badge: A wyvern pierced by a flash of lightning
Motto: Dei auxilio telis meis (By the help of God with my own weapons)
Variant/s: If, VIf
Dates: Sep 1941 to Apr 1945
Role: NF
Theatre(s): MedME, FE

96 SQUADRON
Badge: A lion passant with the constellation Leo
Motto: Nocturni obamblamus (We prowl by night)
Variant/s: IIf, VIf
Dates: Feb 1942 to Aug 1943
Role: NF
Theatre(s): UK

108 SQUADRON
Badge: An oak leaf
Motto: Viribus contractis (With gathering strength)
Variant/s: VIf
Dates: Mar 1943 to Feb 1945
Role: NF
Theatre(s): MedME

125 SQUADRON
Badge: A caribou
Motto: Nunquam domandi (Never to be tamed)
Variant/s: IIf, VIf
Dates: Feb 1942 to Feb 1944
Role: NF
Theatre(s): UK

141 SQUADRON
Badge: On an ogress, a leopard's head
Motto: Caedimus noctu (We slay by night)
Variant/s: If, VIf
Dates: Jun 1941 to Feb 1944
Role: NF
Theatre(s): UK

Above: Target tug RD809 of 34 Squadron at Horsham St Faith, 1949.
Opposite top: Pilots of 68 Squadron in front of Mk.If X7842 'Birmingham Civil Defence', Coltishall, 1942.
Below: A pair of rocket projectile-equipped Beaufighter Xs of 39 Squadron. Note that the one to the left has ASV radar. 39 Squadron Reocrds via Peter Green

143 SQUADRON
Badge: A gamecock attacking
Motto: Vincere est vivere (To conquer is to live)
Variant/s: IIf, XI, X
Dates: Sep 1942 to Oct 1944
Role: TCS
Theatre(s): UK

144 SQUADRON
Badge: In front of a crescent, a boar's head
Motto: Who shall stop us
Variant/s: VI, X
Dates: Jan 1943 to May 1945
Role: TCS
Theatre(s): UK

153 SQUADRON
Badge: In front of a six-pointed star, a bat
Motto: Noctividus (Seeing by night)
Variant/s: If, VIf
Dates: Jan 1942 to Sep 1944
Role: NF
Theatre(s): UK, MedME

167 SQUADRON
Badge: A woodpecker
Motto: Ubique sine more (Everywhere without delay)
Variant/s: TT.10#
Dates: Feb 1953 to Sep 1958
Role: Ferry
Theatre(s): UK and overseas

173 SQUADRON
Badge: A sword grasped by an eagle's claw and a gauntlet
Motto: Quocumque (Whithersoever)
Variant/s: I#
Dates: Apr to Sep 1943
Role: Com
Theatre(s): MedME

176 SQUADRON
Badge: In front of a crescent moon, an eagle's claw holding an Indian dagger
Motto: Nocte custodimus (We keep the night watch)
Variant/s: If, VIf
Dates: Jan 1943 to Jul 1945
Role: NF
Theatre(s): FE

177 SQUADRON
Badge: A cobra entwined in two gun barrels
Motto: Silentur in medias res (Silently into the midst of things)
Variant/s: VIc, X, XI
Dates: May 1943 to Jul 1945
Role: GA
Theatre(s): FE

211 SQUADRON
Badge: A lion ducally crowned
Motto: Toujours a propos (Always at the right moment)
Variant/s: X
Dates: Oct 1943 to Jun 1945
Role: GA
Theatre(s): FE

217 SQUADRON
Badge: A demi shark
Motto: Woe to the unwary
Variant/s: X
Dates: Jun 1944 to Sep 1945
Role: TCS
Theatre(s): FE

219 SQUADRON
Badge: A death's head hawk moth
Motto: From dusk to dawn
Variant/s: If, VIf
Dates: Oct 1940 to Jan 1944
Role: NF
Theatre(s): UK, MedME

227 SQUADRON
Badge: none
Motto: nil
Variant/s: VIc
Dates: Aug 1942 to Aug 1944
Role: TCS, GA
Theatre(s): MedME

235 SQUADRON
Badge: Wyverns spouting fire
Motto: Jaculamur humi (We strike them to the ground)
Variant/s: Ic, VIc, X, XI
Dates: Dec 1941 to Jun 1944
Role: TCS
Theatre(s): UK

236 SQUADRON
Badge: In front of a fountain, a mailed fist grasping a winged sword
Motto: Speculati nuntiate (Having watched, bring word)
Variant/s: Ic, VIc, X
Dates: Oct 1941 to May 1945

Mk.X RD824 of 45 Squadron over Ceylon in 1947.

Role: TCS
Theatre(s): UK

248 SQUADRON
Badge: A sword partly withdrawn from the scabbard
Motto: Il faut en finir (It is necessary to make an end of it)
Variant/s: Ic, VIc, X
Dates: Jul 1941 to Jan 1944
Role: TCS
Theatre(s): UK

252 SQUADRON
Badge: A Spartan shield
Motto: With or on
Variant/s: Ic, VIc, X
Dates: Dec 1940 to Dec 1946
Role: TCS, GA
Theatre(s): UK, MedME

254 SQUADRON
Badge: A raven
Motto: Fluga vakta ok Ijosta (To fly, to watch and to strike)
Variant/s: VIc, X
Dates: Jun 1942 to Oct 1946
Role: TCS
Theatre(s): UK

255 SQUADRON
Badge: A panther's face
Motto: Ad auroram (To the break of dawn)
Variant/s: IIf, VIf
Dates: Jul 1941 to Feb 1945
Role: NF
Theatre(s): UK, MedME

256 SQUADRON
Badge: In front of an anchor, a ferret's head
Motto: Addimus vim viribus (Strength to strength)
Variant/s: If, VIf
Dates: May 1942 to Jan 1943
Role: NF
Theatre(s): UK

272 SQUADRON
Badge: An armoured man
Motto: On, On!
Variant/s: I, VI, XI, X
Dates: Apr 1941 to Apr 1945
Role: GA
Theatre(s): UK, MedME

285 SQUADRON
Badge: In front of a pair of wings, two bird legs
Motto: Respice finem (Consider the end)
Variant/s: I#
Dates: Sep 1943 to Nov 1944
Role: TT
Theatre(s): UK

287 SQUADRON
Badge: A pobjoy perched
Motto: C'est en forgeant (Practice makes perfect)
Variant/s: I#, VI#, X#
Dates: Nov 1944 to Jul 1946
Role: TT
Theatre(s): UK

288 SQUADRON
Badge: A stag
Motto: Honour through deeds
Variant/s: VI#, X#
Dates: Mar to Nov 1944
Role: TT
Theatre(s): UK

307 (POLISH) SQN
Badge: none
Name: Lwowski
Variant/s: IIf, VIf
Dates: Aug 1941 to Feb 1943
Role: NF
Theatre(s): UK

333 (NORWEGIAN) SQUADRON
Badge: In front of a pair of wings, a Viking ship
Motto: For Konge, Fedreland og flaggets heder (For king, country and the honour of the flag)
Variant/s: IIf#
Dates: May to Jun 1943
Role: TS
Theatre(s): UK

515 SQUADRON
Badge: A gauntlet holding a winged dagger
Motto: Celeriter ferrite ut hostes nacsit (Strike quickly to kill the enemy)
Variant/s: II
Dates: Jun 1943 to Feb 1944
Role: ECM
Theatre(s): UK

577 SQUADRON
Badge: none
Motto: nil
Variant/s: I
Dates: Nov 1944 to Jun 1945
Role: TT
Theatre(s): UK

600 SQUADRON
Badge: In front of a crescent, a sword
Motto: Praeter sescentos (More than six hundred)
Variant/s: If, VIf
Dates: Sep 1940 and Feb 1945
Role: NF
Theatre(s): UK, MedME

603 SQUADRON
Badge: On a rock, a triple-towered castle
Motto: Gin de daur (If you dare)
Variant/s: Ic, VIc, X, XI
Dates: Feb 1943 to Dec 1944

OTHER BRITISH BEAUFIGHTER UNITS

Aeroplane & Armament Experimental Establishment
Air-Sea Warfare Air Development Unit
Air Torpedo Development Unit
Anti-Aircraft Co-operation Unit, No.22
Armament Practice Camp, Nos 22, 26, 27
Central Gunnery School
Civilian Anti-Aircraft Co-operation Unit, Nos 1, 2, 3, 4, 5
(Coastal) Operational Training Unit, Nos 2, 3, 5, 6, 9, 132
Conversion Unit, Nos 1330, 1331 and 1692 (Bomber Support) CU

Above: A Beaufighter of 9 (Coastal) Operational Training Unit at Glatton, 1945.
Left: Personnel of 1 Torpedo Trials Unit at Thorney Island, 1947. Both KEC

Heavy Conversion Unit, Nos 1651, 1653, 1668
Empire Central Flying School
Far East Air Force Training Squadron
Ferry Training Unit and the following FTUs: Nos 1, 301, 304, 306 and 307
Ferry Unit, Nos 9, 12
Fighter Interception Unit
Fighter Interception Development Squadron
Flight, Nos 1348, 1435, 1578, 1689, 1692
Gunnery Research Unit
Mediterranean Conversion Flight
Malta Night Fighter Unit
Operational Training Unit, Nos 51, 54, 60
Photo Reconnaissance Unit, No 2
Royal Aircraft Establishment
Signals Development Unit
Signals Flying Unit
Specialised Low Attack Instructors School
Telecommunications Flying Unit
Torpedo Trials Unit, Nos 1, 2
Target Towing Flight at Changi, Seletar, Kai Tak, Abyad

Role: GA
Theatre(s): MedME

604 SQUADRON
Badge: A seax
Motto: Si vis pacem, para bellum (If you want peace, prepare for war)
Variant/s: If, VIf
Dates: Sep 1940 to Apr 1944
Role: NF
Theatre(s): UK

684 SQUADRON
Badge: A mask
Motto: Invisus videns (Seeing through unseen)
Variant/s: VI, X
Dates: Aug to Oct 1945
Role: PR
Theatre(s): FE

695 SQUADRON
Badge: In front of a maunch, three arms in armour
Motto: We exercise their arms
Variant/s: TT.10#
Dates: Dec 1948 to Feb 1949
Role: TT
Theatre(s): UK

FLEET AIR ARM

721 SQUADRON
Badge: none
Motto: nil
Variant/s: II#
Dates: Jul to Nov 1945
Role: FRU
Theatre(s): South Africa

726 SQUADRON
Badge: In front of a wave, a Zulu shield and assegais
Motto: nil
Variant/s: II#
Dates: Jun to Sep 1944
Role: FRU

THEATRE DECODE

UK	United Kingdom and North West Europe
MedME	North Africa and Middle East, Malta, Italy, Mediterranean and Balkans
FE	India, Burma and Malaya
SWPA	SW Pacific, inc Australia, New Guinea and East Indies.
Other areas given in full	

Theatre(s): South Africa

728 SQUADRON
Badge: On a blue field an arrow piercing a target on a Maltese cross
Motto: Descendo discimus (We learn by teaching)
Variant/s: II#, X#, TT.10#
Dates: Feb 1944 to Jun 1946, Jun to Oct 1949
Role: FRU
Theatre(s): MedME

733 SQUADRON
Badge: An eagle in front of two rays of light
Motto: Sursum in nubes (Upwards into the clouds)
Variant/s: II#
Dates: Jan 1944 to Jul 1945
Role: FRU
Theatre(s): FE

762 SQUADRON
Badge: none
Motto: nil
Variant/s: II#
Dates: Mar 1944 to 1945
Role: Trg
Theatre(s): UK

770 SQUADRON
Badge: A cockerel upon clouds
Motto: In alto societas (There's company aloft)
Variant/s: X#
Dates: May 45
Role: FRU
Theatre(s): UK

772 SQUADRON
Badge: In front of a pair of wings, a shepherd's crook and a trident
Motto: none
Variant/s: X
Dates: 1945
Role: FRU
Theatre(s): UK

775 SQUADRON
Badge: none
Motto: nil
Variant/s: II#
Dates: May 1944 to Nov 1945
Role: FRU
Theatre(s): MedME

779 SQUADRON
Badge: On a shield, a battlements above a key
Motto: Finis coronat opus (The end crowns the work)
Variant/s: II#
Dates: Jun 1943 to Aug 1945
Role: FRU
Theatre(s): Gibraltar

781 SQUADRON
Badge: A winged wheel
Motto: Reliability
Variant/s: II#
Dates: Jun to Oct 1943
Role: Trg
Theatre(s): UK

788 SQUADRON
Badge: A target pierced by an arrow in front of two lightning bolts
Motto: Tayari saa yote (Ready all hours)
Variant/s: II#
Dates: Apr 1944 to Jan 1945
Role: FRU
Theatre(s): East Africa

789 SQUADRON
Badge: none
Motto: nil
Variant/s: II#
Dates: Sep 1944 to Nov 1945
Role: FRU
Theatre(s): South Africa

797 SQUADRON
Badge: none
Motto: nil
Variant/s: II
Dates: Mar 1944 to Aug 1945

Role: FRU
Theatre(s): FE

798 SQUADRON
Badge: none
Motto: nil
Variant/s: II
Dates: Oct 1943 to Mar 1944
Role: Trg
Theatre(s): UK

ROYAL AUSTRALIAN AIR FORCE

22 SQUADRON
Badge: On a six-pointed red star, a castle turret pieced by an arrow
Motto: Adsum (Be present)
Variant/s: 31
Dates: Jan 1945 to Aug 1946
Role: FB
Theatre(s): SWPA

30 SQUADRON
Badge: A falcon holding a gauntlet, pieced by a thunderbolt, in its talons
Motto: Strike swiftly
Variant/s: Ic, 31, TT, 31#
Dates: Jun 1942 to 1956
Role: FB, TT
Theatre(s): SWPA, Australia

31 SQUADRON
Badge: none
Motto: nil
Variant/s: Ic, 31
Dates: Sep 1942 to Jul 1946
Role: FB
Theatre(s): SWPA

92 SQUADRON
Badge: none
Motto: nil
Variant/s: 31
Dates: Mar to Sep 1945
Role: FB
Theatre(s): Australia

ROLE DECODE

Com	Communications and Ferrying
ECM	Electronic countermeasures
FRU	Fleet Requirements Unit
GA	Ground Attack
NF	Night Fighter
PR	Photo reconnaissance
TCS	Torpedo/Coastal Strike Fighter
Trg	Training
TT	Target Towing/Calibration

Above: **Mk.VIc JL519 of 227 Squadron, 1943.**
Left: **Arming up V8748 of 96 Squadron at Drem, September 1943.**
Bottom left: **A Mk.X of 177 Squadron over Burma, 1944.**
Bottom right: **A rare colour image of 235 Squadron Beaufighter Ic T4916 'LA-T', 1941.**
All via Andrew Thomas unless noted

93 SQUADRON
- **Badge:** none
- **Motto:** nil
- **Variant/s:** 31
- **Dates:** Jan 1945 to Aug 1946
- **Role:** FB
- **Theatre(s):** SWPA

455 SQUADRON
- **Badge:** Two battle axes and a winged helmet
- **Motto:** Strike and strike again
- **Variant/s:** X
- **Dates:** Dec 1943 to May 1945
- **Role:** TCS
- **Theatre(s):** UK

456 SQUADRON
- **Badge:** none
- **Motto:** nil
- **Variant/s:** IIf, VIf
- **Dates:** Sep 1941 to Mar 1943
- **Role:** NF
- **Theatre(s):** UK

ROYAL CANADIAN AIR FORCE

404 SQUADRON
- **Badge:** A buffalo's head
- **Motto:** Ready to fight
- **Variant/s:** IIF, XI, X
- **Dates:** Sep 1942 to Apr 1945
- **Role:** TCS
- **Theatre(s):** UK

406 SQUADRON
- **Badge:** A lynx leaping
- **Motto:** We kill by night
- **Variant/s:** IIf, VIf
- **Dates:** Jun 1941 to Aug 1944
- **Role:** NF
- **Theatre(s):** UK

409 SQUADRON
- **Badge:** A crossbow superimposed upon a black cloak
- **Motto:** Media nox meridies noster (Midnight is our noon)
- **Variant/s:** IIf, VIf
- **Dates:** Aug 1941 to May 1944
- **Role:** NF
- **Theatre(s):** UK

410 SQUADRON
- **Badge:** In front of a crescent moon, a cougar's face
- **Motto:** Noctivaga (Wandering by night)
- **Variant/s:** IIf
- **Dates:** Apr 1942 to Jan 1943
- **Role:** NF
- **Theatre(s):** UK

ROYAL NEW ZEALAND AIR FORCE

488 SQUADRON
- **Badge:** In front of a taiaha and a tewhatewha, a morepork
- **Motto:** Ka ngarue ratau (We shake them)
- **Variant/s:** IIf, VIf
- **Dates:** Jun 1942 to Sep 1943
- **Role:** NF
- **Theatre(s):** UK

489 SQUADRON
- **Badge:** A kiwi on a torpedo
- **Motto:** Whakatanagata kia kaha (Quit ye like me, be strong)
- **Variant/s:** X
- **Dates:** Nov 1943 to Aug 1945
- **Role:** TCS
- **Theatre(s):** UK

SOUTH AFRICAN AIR FORCE

16 SQUADRON
- **Badge:** An African buffalo riding a rocket (wartime badge)
- **Motto:** Hlaselani (Attack)
- **Variant/s:** X
- **Dates:** Dec 1943 to Jun 1945
- **Role:** FB
- **Theatre(s):** MedME

19 SQUADRON
- **Badge:** An eagle carrying a bomb (wartime badge)
- **Motto:** Swift, silent, sure
- **Variant/s:** X, XI
- **Dates:** Aug 1944 to Jul 1945
- **Role:** FB
- **Theatre(s):** MedME

DOMINICAN AIR FORCE
ESCUADRON DE CAZA-BOMBARDEO
- **Variant/s:** VIf
- **Dates:** 1948 to Jun 1954
- **Role:** FB

ISRAELI AIR FORCE

103 SQUADRON
- **Badge:** An elephant
- **Variant/s:** TF.10
- **Dates:** Jul to Nov 1948
- **Role:** FB

PORTUGUESE NAVAL AIR ARM
ESQUADRILHA B
- **Variant/s:** TF.10
- **Dates:** Mar 1945 to 1949
- **Role:** TCS

TURKISH AIR FORCE
- **Variant/s:** TF.10
- **Dates:** 1947 to 1951
- **Role:** FB

UNITED STATES ARMY AIR FORCE

414TH NIGHT FIGHTER SQUADRON
- **Variant/s:** VIf
- **Dates:** Mar 1943 to Dec 1944
- **Role:** NF
- **Theatre(s):** MedME

415TH NIGHT FIGHTER SQUADRON
- **Variant/s:** VIf
- **Dates:** Feb 1943 to Mar 1945
- **Role:** NF
- **Theatre(s):** MedME

416TH NIGHT FIGHTER SQUADRON
- **Variant/s:** VIf
- **Dates:** Aug 1943 to May 1945
- **Role:** NF
- **Theatre(s):** MedME

417TH NIGHT FIGHTER SQUADRON
- **Variant/s:** VIf
- **Dates:** circa Jul 1943 to May 1945
- **Role:** NF
- **Theatre(s):** MedME

Malta's Auxiliaries

ROBIN J BROOKS DESCRIBES 600 'CITY OF LONDON' SQUADRON'S BRIEF, BUT DECISIVE, DEPLOYMENT TO THE GEORGE CROSS ISLAND

Formed originally from personnel drawn from the banks, the Stock Exchange and similar institutions in the 'square mile' of the City of London, 600 Squadron has a permanent place of honour in the wartime history of Malta. During its brief time on the island, the Auxiliary Air Force unit became a seasoned, and very successful, night predator.

When war broke out, 600 was operating Bristol Blenheim Ifs in the night defence role moving, in turn, to Northolt, Manston, Hornchurch, Catterick and Colerne, and ending up at Predannack in October 1941. While at the Cornish airfield, it converted to the Beaufighter VIf before leaving for a period of intense training for air and ground crews at Church Fenton in Yorkshire.

News filtered through that 600 was due to be posted overseas and in preparation it returned to Cornwall, this time to Portreath. During a three-day stay, the squadron refuelled and was kitted out for overseas. On November 17, 1942, its commanding officer, Wg Cdr Watson, led 17 aircraft to Gibraltar, the journey taking between five and seven hours. After an overnight stop they continued to Blida, Algeria.

Only a few operations were carried out from Blida before switching base to Maison Blanche, Algeria, on

Fg Off 'Togs' Mellersh, a Beaufighter 'ace' with 600 and 96 Squadrons.
via Andrew Thomas

> "NO.600 SQUADRON ARRIVED AT A TIME WHEN MALTA WAS BEGINNING TO HIT BACK AT THE AXIS POWERS."

"A SORTIE WAS A COMBINATION OF PATIENCE, ANTICIPATION AND FRUSTRATION, VERY INFREQUENTLY CROWNED BY TRIUMPH."

Painting another victory marking on the nose of Wg Cdr 'Paddy' Green's (in the cockpit) Beaufighter.
C F Shores
via Andrew Thomas

December 7. On Boxing Day, Wg Cdr C P 'Paddy' Green DSO DFC became CO as the Beaufighters started to make their presence felt. The New Year saw a transfer from Coastal Command to the North Africa Tactical Air Force together with a signal informing Wg Cdr Green that 600 was to relocate to Luqa on Malta.

HITTING BACK

On June 15, 1943 the groundcrew left for Sousse and, on the 23rd, embarked for Malta. The next day, 20 Beaufighters left Bone and settled on the crowded airfield at Luqa. No.600 (City of London) Squadron had joined the Desert Air Force.

Aircrew were billeted in a hotel near Sliema Creek while the rest of the officers were given the 'Meadowbank Hotel' in the town of Sliema. Groundcrew were dispersed throughout the area, some choosing to live in the many yellow stone buildings that abounded along the Luqa perimeter.

No.600 arrived at a time when Malta was beginning to hit back at the Axis powers. After a long period of near starvation and the prospect of surrender, a visit from His Majesty the King on June 23 had inspired both civilians and the military forces on Malta to take the offensive.

'City of London' was tasked with providing an air umbrella over the entire island of Sicily at night. For this, 600 would be supported by one flight from each of 108 and 256 Squadrons.

Having settled in at Luqa, offensive operations started, as 600's operations record book was able to record: "June 26, 1943 – Beau V8757 – Flt Lt Hilken and Plt Off K Lushington. Time up 22:00. Time down 23:15. Patrolled under control of GCI AMES 41 [Ground Controlled Intercept Air Ministry Experimental Station 41] from Luqa climbing to 10,000ft. Nothing contacted or seen."

A night-fighter sortie was a combination of patience, anticipation and frustration, *very* infrequently crowned by triumph. A patrol on June 27 epitomised this cat-and-mouse process. Sqn Ldr Horne AFC and Flt Lt R T Browne were airborne in V8741 from Luqa at 01:20 hours. They were instructed by GCI AMES 804 to climb to 20,000ft (6,096m). Having levelled off, they were handed over to AMES 841 to intercept a 'bogey' identified as flying north-west. At full boost they got within five miles of the target when the GCI lost contact before the Beaufighter's airborne interception (AI) radar could find a trace.

It became obvious to all the aircrew how different circumstances, operational and domestic, were on Malta. Not only was it harder to make contact with the enemy but landing at night was hazardous with just a dim, oil-lit flarepath to guide the pilot. Then it was a desperate search for a weak light mounted on a truck and the almost undistinguishable words 'Follow Me'! During daytime, flying with the constant heat haze making visibility difficult was also new. All of this demanded a high degree of concentration.

Being only 60 miles (96.5km) from Italian-occupied Sicily, Malta was a crucial stepping stone to an invasion of that island. No fewer than 37 squadrons were crammed on Malta and neighbouring Gozo.

Living conditions were primitive and, with a lack of food on the island, 'Malta Dog', a form of dysentery, was prevalent. The early days of July found the 'City of London' drastically depleted due to an epidemic of the 'dog'. With many personnel being taken to Imtarfa Hospital, it became difficult to maintain the eight crews needed for night readiness.

Although it was designed for a two-man crew, it was possible to fit a third person into the Beaufighter's cramped fuselage. By leaving the navigator behind, the powerful twin could be used as a fast 'taxi'. In this role Wg Cdr Green flew Generals Montgomery and Browning to Kairouan in Tunisia, and returned them safely to Malta. The VIPs were involved with planning Operation HUSKY, the Sicilian landings.

Both air and ground crew discovered how best to maximise their day. This began at 06:00, with breakfast being taken at dispersal and work continuing until lunch at 12:30. In the extreme heat of the Maltese summer,

Fitting an engine at dispersal at Luqa.

A 600 Squadron Beaufighter.

"...THE BRIGADIER SAID IT WAS THE MOST MEMORABLE AND THRILLING MOMENT HE HAD HAD SINCE THE WAR BEGAN."

Below, top: Sgt McClean (left) with 600's Engineering Officer, Flt Lt Clenery.

Below, bottom: Groundcrew of 'B' Flight working on a Beaufighter – 20mm cannon in the foreground.

All 600 Squadron archives via author unless noted.

efforts then ceased until 16:30 when preparations began for night flying. If common sense did not prevail, crews quickly discovered that the aircraft were far too hot to work on until the late afternoon.

QUITE A NIGHT

With the invasion of Sicily beginning on July 10, the pace for 600 quickened. Fg Off Turnbull with his navigator, Sgt Fowler, opened the score by destroying a Junkers Ju 88 and watching it fall in flames during an early morning patrol. With a slight reduction in sickness, the squadron was able to fly further sorties enabling the score to steadily climb. On the next night, Sqn Ldr Horne DFC and Fg Off Richie found a lone Heinkel He 111 stooging around Sicily. Firing four two-second bursts they had the satisfaction of seeing it crash near Syracuse.

With the landings proceeding according to plan, a signal was received at Luqa warning 600's personnel to be on four-hour readiness to move into Sicily. Supermarine Spitfire units were already deploying to the island.

The night of July 12/13 saw even further success. From dusk to dawn, 600 – with the aid of the GCI stations, destroyed six enemy aircraft. First to open the night's score were Wg Cdr Green and Fg Off Reg Gillies, shooting down a Ju 88 followed by a He 111.

Shortly after, Fg Offs F R L 'Togs' Mellersh and Armstrong found a Ju 88 just off the coast of Gozo. Although the enemy gunner fought back, the Beaufighter crew soon sent it to a watery grave. Minutes later they were vectored on to an Italian CANT 1007 which was also eliminated.

But the night was still young – Sqn Ldr Hughes with Fg Off Dixon downed a He 111; then Plt Offs Mckinnon and Poole destroyed a Dornier Do 217. It had been, as 600's diarist recorded, "quite a night".

SUSTAINED ATTACKS

With Operation HUSKY several days old, the sustained attacks carried out before the invasion were intensified. British and US bombers from Libya and Tunisia were joining the island's squadrons to keep up the campaign. With a continuous fighter umbrella provided by Malta's fighters for many weeks the Filter Room plotting table at the war rooms, deep in the bastions at Lascaris, was a mass of plots – day and night.

On the night of July 14 Wg Cdr Green again found himself flying in passenger mode. Brigadier Bowen was on board to observe paratroop drops by night. The likelihood of there being 'trade' out there dictated that the CO's usual 'nav', Fg Off Gilles, was also on hand and the guns were loaded.

The call came and Green was vectored to a He 111 just off the Sicilian coast. This was promptly dispatched, to the excitement of the passenger. Landing back at Luqa, the Brigadier said that: "it was the most memorable and thrilling moment I have had since the war began." The following night Green and Gillies shot down four enemy aircraft and damaged a fifth. Minutes later, Fg Off Johnny Turnbull with his navigator, Sgt Fowler, accounted for three Ju 88s with Fg Off Roberts and Flt Sgt Durbaston sending another to the bottom of the sea. This was to prove an all-time record: eight destroyed and one damaged.

As 600 prepared to move into Cassibile on Sicily, the Times of Malta printed the headline: "RAF non-stop attacks. Our fighters yesterday shot down nine aircraft." This included an extract from the squadron diary written by the CO in which he praised the groundcrews: "... to them much of the credit was due for the 'kills' made." By July 25 an advance party had arrived on Sicily and the Beaufighters touched down the next day. Shortly afterwards recognition of 600's contribution came in the form of DFCs for Fg Offs Turnbull, Gillies, Mellersh and Roberts with a DFM going to Flt Sgt Fowler. The 'City of London' had made its mark in the defence of Malta.

KEY MODEL WORLD
Featuring **HORNBY** magazine / **AIRFIX** Model World

YOUR ONLINE SCALE MODELLING DESTINATION

Unmissable modelling inspiration at your finger tips

"*A modeller's paradise*"
Christopher

"*The key that unlocks the world of modelling!*"
Graham

- ✓ Get all the **latest news** first
- ✓ **Exclusive** product and layout videos
- ✓ Fresh **inspiration**, tips and tricks every day
- ✓ More than **5,000 searchable** modelling articles
- ✓ Back issues of **Airfix Model World magazine**
- ✓ Full access to **Airfix Model World** content
- ✓ All available on **any device** - *anywhere, anytime*

Visit: www.keymodelworld.com

A London

Beaufighter VIf X7887 'K-for-King' leading a flight of 600 Squadron, probably while based at Church Fenton, Yorkshire, in September 1942. Close examination of the image shows that the censor has been hard at work, although less than subtly. On 'King' and 'H-for-Harry' the aerials of the airborne interception Mk IV radar have been airbrushed out on the port wings while the 'arrow-head' aerial on the noses has been crudely obliterated. Andrew Thomas - 600 Squadron archive

'Beau'

Beaufighter VIf X7887 was built in late 1941 at the Bristol plant at Weston-super-Mare. It was issued to 600 (City of London) Squadron while it was in the process of converting from Mk.IIs at Predannack in Cornwall. 'K-for-King' stayed with 600 until the unit moved to North Africa in November 1942. It then went on to serve briefly with 153 Squadron at Ballyhalbert, Northern Ireland, while that unit also worked up prior to moving to North Africa. Mk.VIf ended its days with 3 Delivery Flight at High Ercall, Shropshire when it ditched off the Isle of Man on April 18, 1943.

Pete West © 2012

BEAUFIGHTER SURIVORS

Variant	Serial	Location and status
Mk.Ic	A19-43	National Museum of the United States Air Force, Dayton, Ohio, USA. Based upon Fairey-built T5049, supplied to RAAF as A19-43. Other elements from A8-371
Mk.If	X7688	Skysport Engineering, Hatch, Beds, UK. Centre section and forward fuselage, with ex-RAAF rear fuselage. UK registration G-DINT. Long-term restoration project
Mk.XI	A19-144	The Fighter Collection, Duxford, Cambs, UK. Under long-term restoration to fly. Composite using elements of UK-built Mk.XIs A19-144 (ex RAF JM135) and A19-148 (JL946); cockpit from an Australian-built version
Mk.XI	-	Royal Australian Air Force Museum, Point Cook, Victoria, Australia. Composite airframe, stored
TF.X	RD220	National Museum of Flight Scotland, East Fortune, UK. Acquired from South Africa, previously Portuguese BF-10 - see 'Under Other Flags'.
TF.X	RD253	Royal Air Force Museum, Hendon, Gtr London, UK - see panel.
TT.10	RD867	Canada Aviation Museum, Rockcliffe, Ontario, Canada, stored
Mk.21	A8-186	Camden Museum of Aviation, Narellan, New South Wales, Australia. Composite airframe, carries 'Beau-Gunsville' nose-art
Mk.21	A8-328	Australian National Aviation Museum, Moorabbin, Victoria, Australia. Painted as 'A8-39'.

Also: The RAF Museum has an anonymous cockpit section that is believed to come from a Mk.IIf. The Midland Air Museum at Coventry, Warwickshire, UK, has the cockpit of what is believed to be Mk.I T5298. At the Camden Museum of Aviation (see above) the cockpit of Mk.21 A8-386 is displayed with 'Harry's Baby' nose-art. As mentioned in 'Under Other Flags', the remains of TF.X RD448 (D-171) are held at the Israeli Air Force Museum at Hatzerim, Israel.

The RAF Museum's cockpit section was acquired from the College of Aeronautics, Cranfield, Beds, in 1966. KEC

Nearly 6,000 Beaufighters were built, and the pages of this magazine are testament to the aircraft's exceptional contribution to world aviation heritage. So it is a great pity that today there are only nine substantially complete airframes. At Duxford in Cambridgeshire one is under restoration to flying condition, but we will have to be patient for the day when it takes to the skies.

The last time a Beaufighter flew was in 1960 - take a look at *Tugging at Sleeves*. The RAF Museum was still a pipedream in those days and bringing an old airframe all the way back from Singapore to the UK would have been considered prohibitively expensive, with nowhere to show it off. But a couple of years after that, a 'Beau' was firmly on the 'shopping list' for what would become the incredible museum at Hendon.

At Ta Kali airfield on Malta, the remains of TT.10 RD867 were recovered in 1964. Built as a TF.X it was converted to a target-tug before it entered RAF service and ended its days with the Malta Communications Squadron. It was struck off charge on December 11, 1958, and started to decay on the airfield dump. When the hulk was brought back to the UK, it was not a pretty sight. Things did not bode well for bringing a Beaufighter back from the 'dead'.

There was another, far earlier, machine that could be drawn upon. The forward fuselage and centre section of a Mk.I had been used as an engine test-bed at 1 School of Technical Training at Halton, Buckinghamshire. Resting on its undercarriage, with its rear fuselage attached to a shed where controls and instrumentation had been installed, the whole thing represented a surreal prospect. Although the RAF Museum took this on, it was later handed over to Skysport Engineering and forms the basis of a long-term restoration project.

IBERIAN TUTORS

The Lisbon-based Instituto Superior Técnico (technical institute) managed to acquire a pair of former Portuguese naval air arm TF.Xs when they were retired in 1950. They were used in a similar manner to the 'shed' at Halton. Students would learn how to take a Hercules radial off the airframe, determine what 'snag' the instructors had built into it, effect a repair, re-install the engine and get it running.

In July 1965 the institute presented one of these airframes, BF-13, to the RAF Museum and it was moved to Bicester. As it was in much better condition than the former Maltese TT.10, Hendon now had a great chance of achieving not one, but *two* Beaufighter restorations. The Malta target-tug eventually went to Canada in exchange for a Bolingbroke, while BF-13 returned to its 1945 status as RD253. (See the panel for more details.)

The other Lisbon example, BF-10, was moved to Alverca airfield and presented to the Museo do Ar, Portugal's equivalent of the Hendon museum. The 'Beau' was low on the curator's priorities, but high on the South African Air Force Museum's 'wish list'. A deal was struck and the Beaufighter was freighted to Swartkop, near Pretoria, and Supermarine Spitfire IX ML255 travelled in the opposite direction.

By 2000, the SAAF Museum was looking to generate cash for the restoration of a Spitfire to flying condition and BF-10 was offered for sale. At the Museum of Flight at East Fortune, manager Adam Smith reacted with great speed, secured funding from the National Museums of Scotland to the tune of £90,000 and then in double-quick time raised the balance of £100,000 by donations from commerce and the public. On December 12, 2000, TF.X RD220 arrived at East Fortune, the first time the airfield had hosted a Beaufighter since 1946.

AUSTRALIA'S LEGACY

Australia has provided the remainder of the surviving 'Beaus', including

RARE

"THIS IS THE LARGEST AND MOST COMPLEX RESTORATION EVER TAKEN ON BY THE FIGHTER COLLECTION TEAM..."

birds

CONSIDERING ITS ILLUSTRIOUS COMBAT SERVICE, IT IS A PITY THAT SO FEW BEAUFIGHTERS ARE EXTANT

Above: The Fighter Collection's exceptional restoration project, Mk.XI A19-144.
Ken Ellis

Opposite, top: Former Malta target-tug RD867 at Henlow after its restoration. It was delivered to Canada minus its engines.
KEC

Right: TF.X RD253 within the 'Wings over Water' section at the RAF Museum, Hendon. Displayed alongside it is one of the type's 20mm cannon. Key-Duncan Cubitt

Below: Mk.21 A8-186 in 22 Squadron colours at Camden. Tony Hancock via Peter Green

composite airframes that are now at the National Museum of the United States Air Force at Dayton, Ohio, and the RAAF Museum at Point Cook, Victoria. The RAAF Museum's example is not yet on display, but two Australian-built Mk.21s are on show in New South Wales (NSW) and Victoria. (See the feature *Whispering Death* for RAAF 'Beaus' in action.)

The Australian National Aviation Museum at Moorabbin managed to get its Mk.21 to ground-running status in the 1980s and 1990s, but it has not been 'in steam' for some time now. At Narellan, the Camden Museum of Aviation has a complete Mk.21 and the cockpit of another.

The whole Camden example, A8-186, was built by the Department of Aircraft Production during 1945 and was delivered initially to 5 Air Depot at Wagga Wagga, NSW. It operated with 22 Squadron at Moratai, Indonesia, during the closing stages of the Pacific campaign. It was put into store at Wagga Wagga and in 1947 became an instructional airframe.

Offered for disposal in 1949, A8-186 was saved from scrapping when it was purchased by W Strong the following year and it was kept at Boree Creek, NSW. Purchased by the museum in 1965, the restoration presented many problems. Outer wings were tracked down in South Australia, engine cowls in Victoria and other items found in scrap yards all over NSW.

Above: Halton's Beaufighter engine test-rig in October 1961. Roy Bonser-KEC

Right: The starboard Hercules XVIII roaring on the Moorabbin Mk.21 in the late 1980s.

Far right: Rare moment at St Athan in 1969. To the left is TF.X RD253 and to the right, TT.10 RD867, minus engines and ready for shipment to Canada. KEC

BEAUFIGHTER BIOGRAPHY HENDON'S RD253

Oct 1944	Built as a TF.X at Old Mixon, Weston-super-Mare, Somerset.
Nov 2, 1944	Issued to 19 Maintenance Unit, St Athan, Wales, for pre-service installations.
Mar 7, 1945	On charge with 1 Ferry Unit, Pershore, Worcestershire; specialising in the delivery of medium 'twins'.
Mar 18, 1945	Departed to Portela, Lisbon, on delivery to Forças Aéreas da Armada, becoming BF-13 and serving with Esquadrilha 'B'. (See the feature *Under Other Flags* for more.)
circa 1950	Retired and transferred to the Instituto Superior Técnico (technical institute), Lisbon.
Jul 1965	Presented to the RAF Museum and delivered to 71 Maintenance Unit, Bicester, Oxfordshire. The facility started restoration of this airframe and TT.10 RD867. The latter, when completed was presented to Canada in 1969, in exchange for Bolingbroke IVT 10001, now on show at Hendon.
Jan 1967	The project, comprising BF-13 (RD253), elements of RD867 (including the engines) and other parts, transferred to 4 School of Technical Training at St Athan, Wales. Work completed 1968.
Mar 15, 1971	Moved to Hendon and placed on display.

Compiled by Andrew Simpson of the RAF Museum. The museum's exceptional website includes access to exceptionally detailed downloadable histories of each aircraft exhibit. Thoroughly recommended! www.rafmuseum.org

TF.X RD253 at the end of its restoration at St Athan. KEC

"HENDON NOW HAD A GREAT CHANCE OF ACHIEVING NOT ONE, BUT TWO BEAUFIGHTER RESTORATIONS."

SLOWLY BUT SURELY

Of the Australian survivors, the machine that draws all the attention is a long way from home and slowly but surely moving towards airworthiness inside The Fighter Collection's hangar at Duxford in Cambridgeshire. This is *the* largest and most complex restoration ever taken on by the TFC team and it will be several years before it moves under its own power.

This machine is a mixture of British and Australian-built elements. Much of the airframe comes from the centre sections and other parts of two Mk.XIs built at Weston-super-Mare in 1943 and shipped on to the RAAF. Both of these machines (A19-144, RAF serial JM135 and A19-148, previously JL946) were involved in landing accidents at an airstrip at Drysdale, Western Australia, within 18 days of one another, while serving with 31 Squadron.

A report on the incident that befell A19-144 states that the tailwheel collapsed during landing on January 3, 1944, and the pilot retracted the main gear to avoid other aircraft. This all ties in the project's centre section, which is certainly British-built, and damage to the front spar web indicates that the starboard undercarriage either collapsed or was selected up on landing. On January 22, a similar accident occurred to A19-148.

Both machines were struck off charge (on February 1 and March 28 respectively) and stripped of useful components where they lay. Their hulks were discovered and removed from Drysdale in the early 1980s. A decade later they formed the basis of the TFC project.

Although the DAP-built aircraft were essentially facsimiles of British production, various modifications and adaptations were employed. This has provided the restoration crew with more than few conundrums. One of the outer wings is British, the other is Australian. Differences on the 'Oz' versions include: the aileron shrouds being in metal instead of wood and metal; the gun bay doors are metal not wood; pressed nose ribs take the place of the fabricated British type and a it has a different layout to the landing lamp sub-assembly.

Those who make regular visits to Duxford can view progress on this incredible restoration at close quarters. Wisely, nobody at TFC will lay any odds on when A19-144 will fly. Bearing in mind the tale on page 3, *when* this beauty flies will they let it fly down the Champs-Élysées?

WHISPERING DEATH

JIM GRANT DESCRIBES THE EXPLOITS OF AUSTRALIAN BEAUFIGHTERS IN THE STRUGGLE AGAINST THE JAPANESE

While the Royal Australian Air Force may have only had five squadrons equipped with Beaufighters in the Pacific Theatre, they punched well above their weight. Crews had three years of intensive low-level operations over land and sea, hitting the enemy hard; but often at the cost of men and aircraft lost. Combat in the Pacific was a war of grinding attrition.

The two most active RAAF Beaufighter units were 30 and 31 Squadrons, both of which were war-raised. No.30 was formed at Richmond, New South Wales, on March 9, 1942 and five months later 31 was created at Wagga Wagga, NSW.

No.30 remained at Richmond, carrying out conversion and combat training until August 14 when it transferred to the airstrip at Bohle River in Queensland, with the 24 'Beaus' on

UK 'AUSSIE' BEAUFIGHTERS

Two RAAF squadrons flew British-based Beaufighters. No.455 Squadron (illustrated) re-equipped from HP Hampden Is in December 1943 at Leuchars, Scotland. By April 1944, the unit was at Langham, Norfolk and in October 1944 it returned to Scotland, this time to Dallachy. No.455 disbanded there in May 1945.

The other unit was 456 Squadron, which converted from BP Defiant Is to Beaufighter IIs from September 1941 at Valley on Anglesey. No.455 moved on to Mk.VIs in July the following year; taking on DH Mosquito IIs in January 1943.

Beaufighter TF.X NV414 of 455 Squadron RAAF, late 1944.
Pete West © 2012

"POWERFUL, LOW-FLYING AND FAST, THE BEAUFIGHTER BECAME RENOWNED FOR ITS QUIET APPROACH."

No.30 Squadron's A19-120 lifting off from Kiriwina airstrip on Goodenough Island.

strength arriving three days later. After a very brief stay it started moving to Ward's Strip in Port Moresby, New Guinea, on September 8, completing the transfer four days later.

The unit arrived in time to assist in the destruction of enemy troops on the Kokoda Track. In the skies over Burma and in the Pacific, the type's chilling nickname, 'Whispering Death', was used to considerable advantage as propaganda. Powerful, low-flying and fast, the Beaufighter became renowned for its quiet approach. This sobriquet is *said* to have come from the Japanese, but is much more likely to owe its origins to beleaguered Allied troops close to a target zone marvelling at the unheralded approach and the awesome punch of a quartet of 20mm cannons.

CLOSE COMBAT

Japanese landing barges in the Sanananda Point area were the first target for 30 Squadron on September 17, 1942. The excellent results achieved elicited a message from General Douglas MacArthur: "My heartiest congratulations on yesterday's attack on Buna - it was a honey." No.31's Operations Record Book (ORB) described the action:

"Barges on both sides of Sanananda Point and north west [at] Buna Point well strafed, three barges seen burning vigorously, four to five smoking, and many others caught fire, at least 50-percent of barges burned. One small launch [at] Buna strafed, large fire, possibly fuel and stores burning at the beginning of the road at Sanananda, much black smoke and many explosions, smoke seen from 25 miles rising to 2,000ft."

Sanananda and Buna were being used by the Japanese as main supply depots for troops on the Kokoda Track. With the initial absence of Allied air power they had not bothered to camouflage the store dumps properly.

It was a good start, showing the fighting spirit and willingness to get in close with the enemy, qualities that

A 31 Squadron Mk.Ic over the Timor Sea.

AUSTRALIAN NUMEROLOGY

Most unusually for an aircraft in RAAF service, the Beaufighter carried serial numbers in both the A8- and A19- range. The former was applied to Australian-built machines, the latter was applied to the 218 Beaufighter Mk.Ics, VIcs, Xs and XIcs, imported from the UK. The first example, A19-1, was delivered to the RAAF on April 20, 1942 and the last, -218, on August 20, 1945.

Fairey-built Mk.Ic A19-2 was trialled with Wright Cyclone GR-2000-A58 radials as a precaution against a shortage of Bristol Hercules engines. Key-Gordon Swanborough collection

Sqn Ldr D K H Gulliver alongside the rudder of Mk.21 A8-87 of 93 Squadron at Morotai in July 1945 displaying the unit's unofficial badge.

THE GREEN GHOST SQUADRON
R·A·A·F
SPOOKUS SNEAKINUS

> "MACARTHUR: 'MY HEARTIEST CONGRATULATIONS ON YESTERDAY'S ATTACK ON BUNA...IT WAS A HONEY.'"

> "STRIKES BECAME MORE FREQUENT IN JULY 1943 WHEN THE JAPANESE WERE FOOLISH ENOUGH TO TRY MOVING SHIPPING BY DAY."

came to characterise the men of all the Beaufighter units. The unit suffered the loss of its first crew, F/Sgt G W Sayer and Sgt A S Mairet, in British-built Mk.Ic A19-1 on September 23, 1942. September's operational flying amounted to 367 hours. (See the panel for RAAF serial numbers and variants.)

Another machine, A19-68, was downed on October 12 during a low-level strafing run of troops along the Kokoda Track. At this time, the established priority was coastal shipping and offensive sweeps between Buna and Salamaua, the 'milk run' as it was known to the aircrew, plus attacks on the eastern part of the Kokoda Track.

On the 27th eight Beaufighters surprised the Japanese at Lae Harbour and set alight fuel depots on the jetty and round towards Voco Point. On their return, aircrew reported that they could still see the flames from 40 miles (65km) away.

Regarded as an 'unlucky' aircraft, A19-55 was listed as missing off Buna on the 27th. Its pilot had been compelled to land on the airstrip at Gurney, which was barely suitable for even single-engined fighters. The following morning A19-55 and crew returned to base but five days later it was one of two aircraft damaged by Mitsubishi A6M *Zekes* while on a raid.

The outstanding way in which 30 Squadron had carried out its duties during September and October resulted in the award of a DSO to Wg Cdr B R Walker and DFCs to Sqn Ldr R Little, Flt Lt R Uren and Fg Offs Sandford, Spooner, A P McGuire and Campbell. By mid-October operations were transferred to support the fighting on the Owen Stanley Ranges and Salamaua then during November Buna, Amdenba, Sopota and Gona became primary targets. This was the start of the Australian Army's bloody and relentless advance northwards.

No.30 had a particularly busy November,

Above: Mk.VIc A19-77 and Mk.Ic A19-43 plus another in service with 5 Operational Training Unit in December 1942.

Mk.Ic A19-53 named 'Margron' about to touch down at Milne Bay in 1943.

being operational every day the weather permitted, attacking everything Japanese seen on land or sea. Most commonly pairs of Beaufighters combed an area and frequently came back with varying degrees of flak damage, or parts of trees stuck to the leading edges.

BISMARCK SEA

The new year did not start well for 30 Squadron. Mk.Ic A19-55 was destroyed and A19-28, -34 and -73 severely damaged by enemy action on January 2, 1943. From March 2 to 4, the unit took part in the Battle of the Bismarck Sea, the Beaufighters raking eight troopships and escorting destroyers at mast top height while the USAAF bombed from various altitudes above 2,000ft (609m).

Eight Beaufighters strafed the airstrip at Cape Hoskins on September 19 and A19-133 crashed on the return flight. During a sweep over Cape Cunningham on October 2 the 'Beaus' came across a Mitsubishi G4M *Betty* and shot it down. On November 25 bridges around Cape Hoskins were successfully destroyed but the crew of A19-139 perished when it struck tree tops during the attack. In a fast-moving Beaufighter at low-level, the pilot had no chance of taking remedial action if anything went wrong.

The squadron came under control of 71 Wing at Goodenough Island on March 3, 1944, and in June it moved up to Tadji, the former Japanese base which had long been a target the RAAF. Here, 30 Squadron began co-operating the US Navy's torpedo boats

No.31 Squadron A19-43 during 1943.

in the elimination of enemy shipping. July 13 was a bad day: A19-174 crashed into the sea near Buti, A19-146 made a crash-landing at Boram, while A19-185 and its crew simply disappeared, dying unseen as did so many airmen in the vast emptiness of New Guinea and the adjacent ocean and islands.

By October 1944 the unit had transferred to Noemfoor and was striking as far north as Amboina Island. After attacking a truck near Cape Binta in the Celebes, A12-202 crashed into a hillside on December 6.

On January 16, 1945 a headquarters clerical officer, Sgt A S Martin, was awarded the US Soldiers Medal for heroism. In a heavy swell, he swam out from Kiriwina to rescue an American serviceman who was trapped on a rock and in danger of drowning.

No.30 supported the Tarakan landings in May and on June 14 moved on to Sanga Sanga on Morotai for the final two months of the war. With the Japanese surrender, the unit returned to Australia on December 12 and disbanded at Deniliquin on August 15 the following year.

BIT BY BIT

Sqn Ldr B F Rose took command of the second Beaufighter unit, 31 Squadron, on September 1, 1942. On completion of training, it moved briefly to Batchelor airstrip in October 1942, then Coomallie Creek on November 12, both in the Northern Territory. From there, 31 could wage war on Japanese-

No.93 Squadron's A8-149 at Labuan.

DAP BEAUFIGHTERS

The first Australian production Mk.21, A8-1, at Laverton in 1944.

Australia's Department of Aircraft Production obtained a licence to build Beaufighters, but the first was not handed over to the RAAF until May 1944. It was initially intended that the Mk.VII would be chosen for production, but with major improvements being introduced in the UK it was decided that the TF.X, with the Australian designation Mk.21, would be the basis for production.

Ultimately 364 Beaufighters, all carrying A8- serial numbers, were built in factories at Fisherman's Bend and Mascot, with the first DAP aircraft being flown on May 26, 1944 and the last being delivered on November 6, 1945.

Top: **Armourers loading rockets on a 30 Squadron Beaufighter at Noemfoor in 1944.**

Below: **A8-55 of 22 Squadron burning at Sanga Sanga following an accident on June 5, 1945.**

"IN A FAST-MOVING BEAUFIGHTER AT LOW-LEVEL, THE PILOT HAD NO CHANCE OF TAKING REMEDIAL ACTION IF ANYTHING WENT WRONG."

occupied islands across the Timor Sea.

Declared operational on November 17, the unit made its debut with an attack on Moabisse and Boborobi, Timor. It suffered its first casualty when A19-46 crashed into the sea near Cape Batoe Poeti while trying to evade an enemy fighter, killing Sqn Ldr D Riding and W/O R D Clarke.

No.31 stayed in this theatre for two years, destroying Japanese forces bit by bit, before transferring to Noemfoor on November 27, 1944. Its final operational move was to Morotai Island ten days later.

In addition to raids, 31 also escorted convoys in the Timor Sea and had carried out its 100th sortie by the middle of December. Like 30 Squadron, it was an oversized outfit with 24 Beaufighters on its establishment although it often fell below this level due to a lack of replacements. It also carried out strikes in conjunction with 2, 13 (Bristol Beauforts) and 18 Squadron (North American Mitchells).

During early 1943, attacks on barges and escorting convoys continued but on May 6, during a raid on Taberflane on Aroe Island, ten floatplane fighters lined up on a beach were destroyed. Strikes on Tanimbar Island, Langgoer, Penfui and Selaroe became more frequent in July 1943 when the Japanese were foolish enough to try moving shipping by day. No.31 Squadron made life miserable for them, for example on August 17 they caught a vessel in the open, killing the majority of the 50 sailors on board.

On March 8 a lone enemy aircraft got through the defences and destroyed A19-31 and damaged two other Beaufighters on the ground. Penfui was strafed on May 18 and a 'Beau' struck some tree tops but managed to return to base while three others sadly disappeared without trace.

LOVABLE ROCKETS

The unit transferred to Darwin on October 18 and the war continued in the same fashion, but with an increasing number of enemy aircraft and ships being encountered. By the end of 1943, the squadron had carried out 1,137 sorties, and had destroyed 18 aircraft in aerial combat and 49 on the ground, with others claimed as damaged. There was not a lot of glory in 31's war but its sorties meant that no Japanese troops or military facilities were immune from attack.

A break from sorties over enemy territory took place on March 9, 1944, when 14 Beaufighters, accompanied by nine Douglas C-47 Skytrains transporting servicing personnel and equipment, were flown to Potshot in Western Australia to be in place in case a Japanese fleet, seen in the Indian Ocean, turned south towards the Australian coast. No.31 returned to Darwin on the 23rd.

By July 1 Babar, and adjacent Islands, were added to the list of targets and a house, believed to contain senior Japanese officers, was levelled. During August rocket rails were fitted and 31 became the first RAAF Beaufighter squadron to receive these potent weapons. They were first used in action on September 16 when buildings at Naroolia were flattened with ease. The aircrew just loved them. In addition to the 60lb (28kg) rockets, napalm bombs and 325lb depth charges came into service.

The squadron moved to Noemfoor on December 7 and soon after 14 aircraft strafed Jolo Island, a target at the limit of the Beaufighters' range. Through this period there was a steady loss of men and aircraft, however 31 maintained its reputation as always being available for the task in hand. For the first time, all three Beaufighter units, 22, 30 and 31, were in action together.

Following a quiet period during April and May 1945 the tempo again picked up and 31 continued to give close support to the Australian Army until the Japanese surrendered on August 15. By then 31 Squadron had carried out 2,660 sorties with an air combat record of 20 'kills', two 'probables' and 14 damaged. It was not possible to establish how many Japanese soldiers had been killed in strafing attacks nor the number of coastal craft that sank after the unit had departed from the scene.

No.31's last 'op' was on August 3 over Kuching. The unit returned to Deniliquin on December 18 then on to Williamtown on March 12, 1946, and was disbanded on July 6, 1946.

SWEEPING IN PAIRS

The third RAAF unit to fly Beaufighters operationally was 22 Squadron. Having fought the war in New Guinea and the islands to the north with Douglas DB-7s and A-20 Havocs, no serious thought had been given to re-equipping it with Beaufighters. That was until a Japanese raid on its base on Morotai on the night of November 23, 1944, destroyed four aircraft and seriously damaged another

Top: Mk.VIc A19-80 having run off the airstrip into an embankment at Coomallie Creek, December 3, 1943.

Main: Three Mk.21s of 93 Squadron including A8-127 and A8-184.

seven. As the A-20 was being phased out of USAAF service in the Pacific, it was not possible to obtain replacements so Beaufighters were chosen.

It was not until February 11, 1945, that the squadron recommenced operations with a full establishment. That day the unit's ORB described how eight aircraft carried out a: "search of southerly escape route [with] particular attention [to the] Padi area, strafed and hit light house and radar station, damaged camouflaged transformer."

The most common 'ops' were carried out by pairs and consisted of armed reconnaissances, coastal shipping sweeps, and attacks on bridges. Additionally, pamphlets urging the Japanese to surrender were dropped.

Mk.Ic A8-43, crewed by Fg Off Collet and Flt Lt Frances, went into the sea on February 28. They managed to get a message out and were rescued by an air-sea rescue Consolidated Catalina.

Operations in March continued as before, with pairs marauding over Japanese territory and destroying everything that moved or was inadequately camouflaged. The ORB for the 30th stated that A8-27, -42, -115 and -118: "took part in a dawn attack on Liang airstrip on Amboina Island and Beaufighter A8-115, pilot W/O W J Hart, encountered heavy anti-aircraft fire and was hit in both legs. After assistance from the navigator in steadying the aircraft while the pilot applied emergency bandages to his legs and despite severe pain and loss of blood, he flew the aircraft for 2½ hours across 350 miles of ocean and made a perfect landing at the base."

No.22 arrived at Tawi Tawi in the Philippines on May 22. Moving to Morotai allowed it to provide air cover for the Australian landings at Labuan and Brunei and it finished its war in this area.

Most of the post-surrender flying in September was reconnaissance over the Celebes and Ambon. A C-47, with ten members of the squadron on board, ditched in the sea on the 19th 'but 16 hours later they were rescued by a Royal Australian Navy launch. No.22 Squadron returned to Australia on December 17 and disbanded on August 25, 1946.

OCCUPYING FORCES

Two more squadrons, 92 and 93 were formed in 1945, but only the latter became operational, briefly, before the end of the war in the Pacific. No.93 'Green Ghost' was formed at Kingaroy, Queensland, on January 22, 1945, and when training was complete on June 13 it was transferred to Labuan Island. Due to the unsuitability of the runways at both airfields and it was not until August 5 that Beaufighters arrived, officially beginning 'ops' two days later.

However, the ORB reports on July 26 that: "two aircraft had preceded the rest of the squadron [to Labuan] on escort duty. They escorted Spitfires to Labuan and were ordered to remain. These aircraft attacked a hotel at Sibu, Borneo, and destroyed it with rockets. It was believed that there was a conference of Japanese officers at the hotel."

No.93 carried out armed reconnaissances of Rjanag, Mukan, Bintula and Sibu and rocket attacks. Its last two operations were carried out on August 13 when five aircraft strafed the airfield at Tromboul while others flew to Kuching to check out the airfield for enemy activity.

Stood down from operations on August 15, the next three weeks were spent locating and dropping leaflets on Japanese personnel. Then followed a series of meteorological

"W/O W J HART ENCOUNTERED HEAVY ANTI-AIRCRAFT FIRE AND WAS HIT IN BOTH LEGS. ...DESPITE SEVERE PAIN HE MADE A PERFECT LANDING AT THE BASE."

Above: **The last British-built Beaufighter delivered to the RAAF, A19-218, at Pearce in Western Australia late in 1945.**

flights and finally 93 escorted the aircraft of 81 Wing to join the British Commonwealth Occupation Force in Japan. On December 20 the squadron began transferring to Narromine where it was reduced to a cadre and finally disbanded on August 22, 1946.

The last unit, 92 Squadron, was designated as a ground-attack unit and was formed at Kingaroy, Queensland, on May 25, 1945. Its first Beaufighter was delivered on July 4 although it had previously received an Avro Anson on June 19 and a Bristol Beaufort on the 20th. Minimal flying was carried out during 92's first two months but gradually the unit built up to full strength.

Still not operational at the end of the war, 92 lost no aircrew in action but on September 3, a Beaufighter flown by W/O Jorgensen crashed at Narrandra, killing himself and six men on the airfield. After a brief life, 92 Squadron formally ceased to exist on January 4, 1946.

Beaufighters remained in service after the end of World War Two with 30 (Target Towing) Squadron, formed on March 8, 1948. This unit retained them until it was disbanded on March 21, 1956. The RAAF's last Beaufighters, Mk.21s A8-357 and -363, were transferred to Woomera in South Africa to take part in missile trials. The last example in RAAF service, A8-357, was taken out of service on December 10, 1957.

ACKNOWLEDGEMENTS

All images courtesy of the RAAFA Aviation Historical Museum of Western Australia unless noted.

UNDER OTHER FLAGS

DOUG HALL OUTLINES OVERSEAS USE AND POST-WAR EXPORTS

Australian Mk.21 A8-285 of 30 (Target-Tug) Squadron at East Sale, 1952.
RAAFA Aviation Historical Museum of Western Australia via Jim Grant

Despite its proven track record, ease of maintenance and its reliable Hercules engines, what could have been a vibrant export market for Beaufighters failed to materialise. Only three countries directly opted for the type, while a third acquired a handful through a clandestine route. Two of these nations used them in anger.

During the war, four Commonwealth air forces flew 'Beaus': Australia (five squadrons in the Pacific, two in the UK), Canada (four in the UK), New Zealand (two in the UK) and South Africa (two in the Middle East). As charted in the feature *Whispering Death*, Australia also built the type under licence. Other than the RAAF, the rest swiftly disbanded their fleets; Australia soldiering on in the target facilities role until December 1957. (See the *Squadron Directory* for more details of Commonwealth usage.)

With no capable night-fighter on the horizon, the USAAF turned to the Beaufighter as a stop-gap as detailed in *Stars and Stripes*. With the advent of the exceptional Northrop P-61 Black Widow, the surviving American 'Beaus' were returned to the RAF.

Production of Beaufighters came to a halt in the UK in September 1945 and two months later in Australia. This was not the case with its 'rival', the de Havilland Mosquito, which continued to be churned out until 1950 and had the advantage of large numbers in storage to act as sources of spares. The wooden structure scored against the 'Mossie' in some climates, but its side-by-side cockpit gave it more appeal as a night-fighter and crew trainer.

As related in the article *Tugging at Sleeves*, the RAF very rapidly wound down its Beaufighter squadrons, quickly consigning aircraft to scrapheaps. Although the RAF enjoyed great longevity with the type - retiring the last target-tugs in 1960 - the font of airframes for possible export was nowhere near as large as that of the Mosquito. Nevertheless, British-based maintenance units held significant stocks, many 'zero-time' with no service use in their documentation.

CARIBBEAN

Four RCAF squadrons flew Beaufighters during World War Two. TF.X NE355 of 404 Squadron, based at Davidstow Moor, Cornwall, 1944.
Pete West © 2012

COMBATANTS

Occupying the eastern end of the huge Caribbean island of Hispaniola (its neighbour is Haiti) the Dominican Republic may seem an unusual customer for British aircraft. In 1948 the Fuerza Aérea Dominicana went on a shopping spree in the UK, acquiring five Mosquito FB.VIs and ten Beaufighter TF.10s (serials 306 to 315).

The TF.10s were refurbished by Bristol at Filton and supplied complete with rocket rails. Hercules XVIs were installed, effectively bringing them to Mk.VI status. Deliveries were completed by October 1948 and the 'Beaus' joined the Escuadrón de Caza-Bombardeo at San Isidoro.

Since 1930 Dominica had been in the clutches of the ruthless dictator General Rafael Trujillo, known as 'El Jefe' (The Boss). In May 1961 he perished in a hail of bullets, but in the decades preceding, he survived several assassination attempts and brutally suppressed a series of invasions and coups.

On June 14, 1949 a very unusual liberation force approached Dominica – the so-called 'Luperon Invasion'.

Beaufighter TF.10 310 touches down somewhere in the USA on delivery to Dominica in the autumn of 1948. Key-Gordon Swanborough collection

"BEAUFIGHTERS AND MOSQUITOS STRAFED AN ALREADY DAMAGED CONSOLIDATED CATALINA LYING IN AN INLET NEAR PUERTA PLATA..."

Portuguese TF.10 BF-10 at Lisbon in the early 1960s. It is now at the National Museum of Flight Scotland, East Fortune. Peter Green collection

Sources vary, but up to 14 'seaplanes' carrying armed exiles landed on the northern shores to the west of Puerto Plata. Beaching some of the aircraft on the fabulous golden sands of the resort at Luperon, the small force hoped to rally support as is went along.

This motley group was promptly routed and on the 20th Beaufighters and Mosquitos strafed an already damaged Consolidated Catalina lying in an inlet near Puerta Plata; killing at least a dozen rebels. This was not the last time Beaufighters were action; as related in *Tugging at Sleeves*, the RAF employed TF.10s against insurgents in Malaya until the end of 1949.

FILM STARS

Post-war, Britain was keen to pull out of Palestine and in November 1947 the United Nations declared that the region should be partitioned, allowing for both Palestinian and Zionist states to be established. On May 14, 1948, the State of Israel was proclaimed an immediately found itself facing oblivion as Egypt, Syria, Jordan, Lebanon and Iraq pledged its destruction.

For some time, Jewish settlers had been building up a rag-tag of aircraft to form the Heyl ha'Avir, the Israel Defence Force/Air Force. In April 1947 Fairey Aviation at Ringway (now Manchester Airport) put six Beaufighter TF.10s on the British civil register (G-AJMB to 'G, previously RAF RD135, RD448, RD427, ND929, NV306 and LZ185 respectively) and started refurbishing them. Out went the cannons and other military equipment and in went

Hercules XVI radials, in a similar manner to the Dominican machines.

The 'Beaus' were apparently destined for use in a film and on July 21, 1948, the half-dozen aircraft were re-registered to Robert Dickson and partners of York Street, London W1. The contract was valued at £9,000 – a cool £270,000 in present-day values – and the aircraft were ferried to Thame in Oxfordshire.

On arrival G-AJMF (formerly NV306) was stripped for spares. With the Israeli War of Independence raging and combat-capable aircraft being acquired by fair means or foul for the IDF/AF, British customs and intelligence personnel were more than a little fascinated by the Thame Beaufighters, maintaining a close watch.

Tragedy struck on July 28 when *Mike-Echo* (the one-time ND929) crashed near the airfield, killing its pilot. That brought still more unwanted attention to the 'film set'. The following day, the four remaining 'stars' were to carry out a full-blooded stream take-off for the benefit of the cameras and then fly to 'Scotland' where the rest of the movie was to be made.

No film was ever released; the Beaufighters did not fly north. Instead, by September they were on charge with 103 Squadron at Ramat David and having 20mm cannon installed. They had forsaken their British registrations for the Israeli serials D-170 to -173.

On October 15 two were in action at El Arish. Four days later, D-171 attacked an Egyptian ship. In 1944 and 1945, when it was RD427, it had served with 404 Squadron RCAF and then 455 Squadron RAAF when anti-shipping strikes were its bread and butter. An Egyptian Hawker Fury intercepted and while D-171 was taking evasive action, the Centaurus-powered fighter crashed into the Mediterranean, killing its pilot.

The fortification at Iraq Suweidin, near Ashdod, was raided by a pair of 'Beaus' on October 20. One of them, D-171, was hit by anti-aircraft fire and crashed, killing the three on board. The remains of this machine were salvaged in the 1990s and are now at the Israeli Air Force Museum at Hatzerim.

Eleven days after D-171 was downed, a truce was declared, although fighting flared up from time to time until a final armistice was declared in July 1949. By that time, Beaufighters D-170 and D-172 were still on the IDF/AF inventory, but probably long since flightless. They were scrapped the following year.

MARITIME PATROLLERS

In 1943 Portugal took delivery of Blenheim IVs for maritime patrol by the naval air arm, the Forças Aéreas da Armada. These veterans were replaced by surplus Beaufighter TF.10s and the first of 16 were ferried to Portela, near Lisbon, in March 1945. Given the serials BF-1 to BF-16, they were joined by another (BF-17, previously RD862) in April 1946, supplanting one of the originals that had been written off in October 1945.

Serving with Esquadrilha 'B', the Portuguese Beaufighters flew on until 1950 and several became staples of the world's surviving population of the breed – see the feature *Rare Birds*. Bizarrely, the 'Armada' Beaufighters were replaced by Curtiss SB2C Helldivers of much the same vintage.

During 1944, Turkey received some Beaufighters from RAF Middle Eastern stock and in 1946 ordered a batch of 24 reconditioned TF.10s. Deliveries were completed in 1947 and they are thought to have been retired by 1950. Along with the TF.10s, a pair of Beauforts was also dispatched, to act as a conversion trainers. These two were the only examples of the type to be exported.

> "BIZARRELY, THE ARMADA BEAUFIGHTERS WERE REPLACED BY CURTISS SB2C HELLDIVERS OF MUCH THE SAME VINTAGE."

Above: **A Turkish TF.10, believed to be RB698, at Blackbushe, Hampshire, in March 1947 on delivery.** Key-Gordon Swanborough collection

Below: **A Beaufighter captured by the Italians and hastily painted up in Regia Aeronautica markings at Catania, Sicily, in 1942.** Peter Green collection

VISIT OUR ONLINE SHOP

shop.keypublishing.com/Luftwaffe

Key Shop

Originally published in 2014, this popular special examines the Luftwaffe of World War Two right from the invasion of Poland in September 1939.

The men and machines of Nazi Germany's airborne armada led Hitler's blitzkrieg across Europe and then into the heart of the Soviet Union.

Throughout these momentous years, the Luftwaffe's pilots found themselves at the controls of cutting-edge warplanes, culminating in jets far ahead of anything the Allied forces could muster.

Luftwaffe Eagles is a 100-page special packed with first-hand accounts, features by leading aviation writers, glorious artwork, and contemporary photos.

Prepared by the editorial team that brings you Britain's top-selling aviation monthly, FlyPast, this is a highly collectable tribute to a formidable air force.

ONLY £8.99 + FREE P&P*

SUBSCRIBERS don't forget to use your **£2 OFF DISCOUNT CODE!**

IF YOU ARE INTERESTED IN **HISTORIC AVIATION** YOU MAY ALSO WANT TO ORDER…

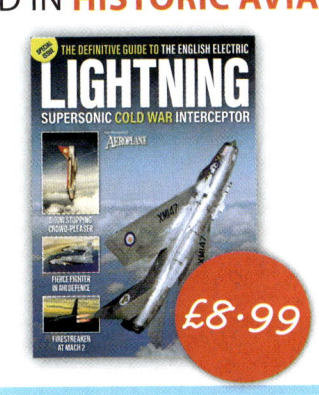

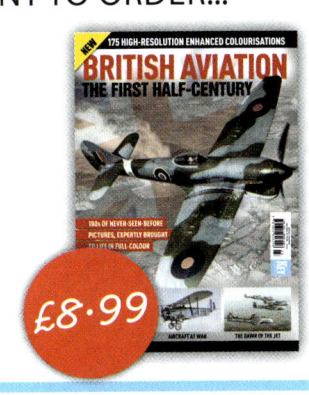

- Cold War Warriors — £8.99
- Lightning — £8.99
- Wellington — £8.99
- British Aviation — £8.99

FREE P&P* when you order online at…

shop.keypublishing.com/Luftwaffe

Call +44 (0)1780 480404 *(Monday to Friday 9am-5.30pm GMT)*

Also available from **W.H Smith** and all leading newsagents.

*Free 2nd class P&P on all UK & BFPO orders. Overseas charges apply.

IN 1941 THE BEAUFIGHTER WAS THE MOST HEAVILY ARMED FIGHTER ANYWHERE. WE PRESENT A PORTFOLIO OF ITS FORMIDABLE ARSENAL

Above, left: **The cannon installation in the lower fuselage allowed for ease of access for the armourers.** Peter Green collection
Above, middle: **Close up of the torpedo shackles and connectors under the centre section. The crew entry door is open.**
Above, right: **A torpedo loaded under a 'Torbeau'. Note the radar aerial under the nose.** Peter Green collection
Below: **A D-Day striped TF.X with 250lb bombs under wing.**

Above: **Armourers loading rocket projectiles on to the under wing launchers. Prior to take-off, armourers pulled lanyards to render the projectiles live.** KEC

Right: **A view of the launch rails and the 'pallet' they were mounted on.** Peter Green collection

WEAPON TRIALS

During the spring of 1941 two Merlin-engined Mk.IIs (R2274 and R2306) were converted to Mk.V status. For this only two 20mm cannon in the lower fuselage were retained and a Boulton Paul BPA.I gun turret was positioned just behind the cockpit, fitted with four Browning machine-guns. The observer's cupola was replaced by a flush glazing. No other Mk.Vs were converted.

Various schemes were examined to put more powerful guns into the Beaufighter. Adapting a 2lb anti-tank field gun or a 2lb gun from a light tank turret was considered and much development work went into making the 40mm Bofors anti-aircraft gun an airborne weapon. Vickers and Rolls-Royce separately came up with purpose-designed 40mm guns and Beaufighter prototype R2055 was converted to carry the Vickers product in the starboard lower fuselage and the Rolls-Royce version to starboard. Trials, carried out from Duxford, went well and the Vickers gun was deemed the best choice. In the end, the Beaufighter was not destined to carry this weapon in anger; Hawker Hurricanes were adapted to carry one under each wing.

One of two Mk.V trials machines, R2274 with the turret installed just behind the cockpit. Note the strengthening strips below the turret. Key Gordon Swanborough collection

Below: **Rocket armed TF.X with faired-over cannon ports and a 200-gallon ferry tank under the centre section.**

Middle, left: **Mk.VI EL223/G with under-slung torpedo. The '/G' suffix to the serial number denoted that the aircraft was to be permanently under guard when parked up. This machine served all of its time with the Torpedo Development Unit at Gosport.**
Key-Gordon Swanborough collection

Middle, right: **A pair of 250-pounders on the centre fuselage bomb cradle.**
Peter Green collection

Bottom: **A Beaufighter showing the large gun ports in the lower fuselage.** KEC

BEAUFIGHTER ARMAMENT

Mk.VIf fighter:	4 x 20mm Hispano cannon mounted in the lower fuselage 6 x 0.303in machine-guns, four grouped in the starboard wing, two grouped in the port wing 2 x 250lb (113kg) bombs on a carrier under the centre section
Mk.X strike fighter:	4 x 20mm Hispano cannon mounted in the lower fuselage 1 x 0.303in machine-gun in the rear fuselage gun position; earlier machines often fitted a Vickers K-gun in this position 1 x 1,650lb (748kg) 18in (45.7cm) British torpedo or a 2,127lb 22½in US torpedo, mounted on shackles under the centre section. Or... 8 x 60lb rocket projectiles carried on four-rail launchers under each wing, plus 2 x 250lb bombs on a carrier under the centre section. Or... 2 x 500lb bombs on a carrier under the centre section and 2 x 250lb on wing pylons
Mk.21 strike fighter:	4 x 20mm Hispano cannon mounted in the lower fuselage 4 x 0.5in machine-guns, two in each wing 8 x 90lb rocket projectiles carried on four-rail launchers under each wing, plus up to 1,000lb of bombs under the centre section

A BOB'S WORTH

"ONE OF THE BEST HATED MACHINES ON THE LUFTWAFFE LIST."

A BOOKLET PUBLISHED IN 1944 PAID TRIBUTE TO AN AIRCRAFT THE PUBLIC WERE NOT THAT FAMILIAR WITH. JONATHAN GARRAWAY TREASURES HIS COPY

Taken over, merged, renamed: the company is long gone but in its time Gale and Polden of Argyll Street in London and Aldershot were prodigious printers and publishers. During the war a series of small, well-illustrated booklets appeared produced on 'austerity' paper and covering a wide range of military subjects.

While they were informative, they were designed to boost morale and spread propaganda. One wonders what German intelligence would have made of a copy. For the wartime reader, excitement was heightened by black bars 'censoring' some words or even sections, providing a thrill that this really was cutting-edge stuff!

My copy of the ponderously-titled *Beaufighter - The Account of the Part Played by the Aircraft in Defence and Offence* had seen its fair share of 'flak' damage but at £3 I thought it well worth it. Published in 1944, it sold for a shilling, or a 'bob', as it was colloquially known. (A shilling was written as 1/- and is 5p in present-day coinage.) Today, these little tomes are all highly collectable.

Compiled by R H H Macaulay, Beaufighter is an assembly of essays on aspects of the big twin's exploits. Sometimes it uses direct quotes from aircrew, but mostly adopts the 'flowery' narrative that newsreels and official releases brimmed with in those days. Macaulay sets the scene, explaining that the Beaufighter: "first hit the German during the night Battle of Britain, and has been hitting where it hurts most ever since."

Starting with the faltering nocturnal combats of September and October 1940, with each turn of the page the reader is taken on a tour-de-force of the Beaufighter's many capabilities: Western Desert, cat-and-mouse of Ground Controlled Interception (GCI), the jungles of Burma to the Strike Wings and mast-top assaults.

For a wartime publication it is full of dates, *some* mention of bases (mostly

> "...THE BEAUFIGHTER: FIRST HIT THE GERMAN DURING THE NIGHT BATTLE OF BRITAIN, AND HAS BEEN HITTING WHERE IT HURTS MOST EVER SINCE."

of the 'Hampshire' or 'southerly' nature), and *very* specific on enemy ground targets and vessels. Aircrew names are *not* given, not even of the 'Jim' and 'Ted' variety. Unit numbers are also taboo, though 600 Squadron is referred to as the 'City of London night-fighter squadron'.

Most striking are plentiful statistics throughout and there is a very detailed section giving performance figures, weights, disposable load, fuel tankage and more. Sometimes this brings the 'censor's' black pen out, for example: "although the addition of a torpedo reduced the cruising speed of the Beaufighter ▬▬▬ as soon as the 'tin fish' was clear the speed was stepped up from the torpedo-releasing speed of 200mph to the normal 330mph."

BEAUFIGHTER 'BANTER'

While describing a GCI encounter, a good sample of the 'banter' between pilot and control is given. "You are getting close. You ought to bounce one in a minute or two. But there are some of ours about, so watch out!" Then, in the pilot's words: "Everything happened. A dark shape to the right and slightly above. I thought, 'Hurricane night-fighter'; then 'By God, it might have been a Hun!'"

There is an explanation of the coining of the nickname 'Whispering Death': a Japanese prisoner of war who described the sound of 'Beau' as: "a peculiar whistling whisper." Macaulay quotes a pilot after strafing a parade of Japanese soldiers: "As I pressed the button, I was surprised to see that they were still standing to attention: they couldn't have heard us."

The audacious flag-dropping sortie to Paris is prominently featured. The unnamed pilot thought the navigation not too arduous: "We could see the Eiffel Tower when we were 30 or 40 miles from Paris..." Low over the city, he asked his observer if he was ready: "Yes, I'm ready all right, but the slipstream is nearly breaking my arm." The furled flag was pushed down the flare chute and history was made.

While discussing the Beaufighter's ability to take a lot of damage and still get home, Macaulay writes about *F-for-Freddie*, which was considered a 'jinx'. When it arrived on squadron, it disgraced itself with a belly-landing. But it went on to carry ten 'kill' markings and clock up 220 hours without further mishap.

Freddie was not cursed: "It had the reputation of being the fastest aircraft on the squadron, and those swastikas are mute evidence of its airworthiness, its speed and the deadly accuracy of its guns and last, but by no means least, of the skill of the pilots."

No wonder the 'Beau' was: "One of the best-hated machines on the Luftwaffe list."

Beaufighters of 254 Squadron at work, September 1944. Author's collection

Left: The cover of *Beaufighter*, a good bob's worth!

Right: Look carefully and there are two Beaufighters amid the chaos in a raid on trawlers off the French coast in August 1944. A salvo of rockets can be seen to the left and right. Author's collection

Strike

AFTER A FALTERING START, NORTH COATES PROVED THE BEAUFIGHTER TO BE A LETHAL ANTI-SHIPPING WEAPON AS GRAHAM PITCHFORK EXPLAINS

Coastal Command's campaign against enemy surface shipping during the early years of the war met with limited success. The Blenheims, Hampdens and Beauforts rarely attacked as a co-ordinated force and, faced by a formidable threat,

With a torpedo under its belly, a Beaufighter TF.X tucks up the gear. Note the venturi tube under the wing which worked the bellow-like dive brakes. Bristol-KEC

TF.X RD853 of 254 Squadron, North Coates, 1944.
Pete West © 2012

Below: A Beaufighter at the moment of torpedo release.

Bottom: Aircrew of 254 Squadron with Bill Sise in the centre and Del Wright on his left.

suffered heavy losses for very modest results.

The availability of the Beaufighter brought about a dramatic change in the anti-shipping campaign and the Command's Strike Wings changed the course of the war in the waters off German-occupied Europe.

In November 1942 the first of the Strike Wings was formed at North Coates on the Lincolnshire coast. Its task was to attack the important convoys, heavily escorted by flak-ships, transporting raw materials from Scandinavia to the Dutch port of Rotterdam. It consisted of two squadrons of Beaufighter VIcs: 236 armed with cannon, machine-guns and bombs and 254 with cannon and torpedoes.

The first operation was mounted on November 20 to attack a southbound convoy off the Hook of Holland. Twenty-five Beaufighters took off with New Zealander, Sqn Ldr G D 'Bill' Sise leading the torpedo-carrying flight of nine 254 'Torbeaus'. One of the youngest pilots on the sortie was 236's Sgt David Ellis with his observer Eric Ramsbottom. Their 'Beau' was armed with cannon and two 250lb (113kg) bombs as part of the anti-flak force.

The fighter escort failed to make the rendezvous and the force headed across the North Sea. The formation split up and Ellis' section hit the Dutch coast to the south of the convoy and was unable to make an attack at the briefed time. Meanwhile, German fighters pounced repeatedly on Sise's flight. His aircraft was badly damaged but he limped home to make a crash-landing near Frinton-on-Sea. For his gallantry on this first ill-fated raid he was awarded the DFC.

PUT TO THE TEST

This first 'op' by the Strike Wings was a tragic failure resulting in the loss of three crews, five aircraft and others badly shot up. Among those lost were the CO of 236 Squadron and one of his flight commanders. Within days, Wg Cdr Neil Wheeler arrived to take command.

Wheeler, 26, was a graduate of the RAF College at Cranwell and one of the pioneer Spitfire photographic reconnaissance pilots; his exploits during 56 operations earned him the DFC. On arrival he recognised the low morale and immediately reviewed and revised the tactics. To provide stronger support for the 'Torbeaus', 143 Squadron joined the Wing in the New Year in the anti-flak role.

Wheeler recommended that the three units should attack together and established a period of intense training in which everyone was expected to match his high standards. During February some crew flew more than 20 sorties practising tactical formations and co-ordinated strikes.

Wheeler was adamant that a fighter escort was essential and vowed that no matter how much pressure was put on him, he would refuse to lead a sortie without an escort.

Wheeler's firm views, natural leadership and example brought an enthusiastic response from his crews. He was soon recognised as a strict but fair man, a trait that remained with him throughout his long RAF career. Finally, on April 18, 1943, his beliefs, intensive training and new tactics were put to the test. An important and heavily-defended convoy had been sighted off the Dutch coast and Wheeler was ordered to attack.

Six machines from each of 143 and 236 Squadrons, armed with four 20mm cannon and a pair of 250-pounders, were to take on the flak-ships. Nine 'Torbeaus' of 254, led by Bill Sise, were to hit the merchant ships.

David Ellis flew as No.2 to his 236 Squadron Flight Commander, Sqn Ldr 'Dusky' Denholm. The Beaufighters took off at 13:20 hours and Ellis settled in alongside Denholm as they crossed the Wash, heading for Coltishall where they saw their fighter escort taking off. Wheeler led the 21 Beaufighters, and their escort of 30 long-range fighters, across the North Sea at 50ft (15m).

Bob Irving, Wheeler's navigator, set a good course; his timing and plotting were perfect and after 40 minutes, Ellis saw Wheeler start a climbing turn to 1,500ft as the convoy came into view. Eight merchant ships sailing in two lines of four were protected by six escorting flak-ships with two minesweepers ahead.

Ellis selected his target as radio silence was broken and Wheeler ordered: "Attack, attack, attack!" The formation turned to starboard, the 'Torbeaus' remaining at low level as the dozen anti-flak 'Beaus' dived into the fray.

Ellis commented: "As I settled into the dive I brought my gun sight to bear on the target and saw cannon shell splashes in the sea move towards the ship. At the same time tracer shells were rising to meet me. At the last moment, with my sight still on the ship, I released my two bombs and skimmed over it and weaved my way through the convoy."

As the anti-flak force unleashed cannons and bombs, Sise led the others, each armed with a Mk.XV torpedo and four cannons, low down against the major merchant ships. Flying in

> **"WHEELER'S FIRM VIEWS, NATURAL LEADERSHIP AND EXAMPLE BROUGHT AN ENTHUSIASTIC RESPONSE FROM HIS CREWS."**

been left burning and badly damaged. It was completed in four minutes and without loss. All the Beaufighters returned safely and the raid was recognised as an outstanding success.

Left: Wg Cdr Neil Wheeler, CO of 236 Squadron. With the permission of Commandant RAF College Cranwell

CANNON AND TORPEDOES

The Wing was next in action on April 29 after a 143 Squadron Beaufighter flying a LAGOON reconnaissance sortie sighted a convoy of six merchant vessels and nine escort ships off the Netherlands. Following a detailed crew briefing, the Wing was airborne at 16:50 with Wheeler in the lead. On this occasion it consisted of 12 'Torbeaus' of 254, nine 'Beaus' of 236 with bombs and six of 143 with cannons. The force was escorted by 24 Spitfires and six Mustangs.

The ships were located off Texel. Three minesweepers in line abreast were leading the merchant vessels in two lines astern. Escort craft were stationed around the convoy. Five balloons at about 800 to 1,000ft were picketed from the centre ships. The disposition of the escorts made the target more formidable than the previous one. Also, owing to a change in speed by the enemy since the last recce, the all-important element of surprise was lost. However, Wheeler's

> **"...AN OUTSTANDING LEADER WITH COOL COURAGE AND INFECTIOUS CONFIDENCE."**

A Mk.VIc 'Torbeau'.

his formation was another young pilot, recently commissioned 'Del' Wright who had joined in June 1942 with his observer Bob Price - they had been together since their days on Blenheims.

Flying in pairs at 120ft, the 'Torbeaus' headed for the freighters and released their torpedoes at 800 yards range. Despite the intense anti-aircraft fire, Wright had a perfect run to the 4,900-ton Norwegian *Hoegh Carrier* and released his torpedo. Although individual pilots did not observe the progress of their weapons as they took evasive action immediately after the drop, following crews saw definite hits.

Analysis indicated that three torpedoes had hit, including Wright's, which had struck between amidships and the stern. It was later confirmed that the *Hoegh Carrier* had sunk and other ships had

> "HIS SKILFUL LEADERSHIP BROUGHT THE ATTACKERS INTO POSITION AND THE ONSLAUGHT BEGAN."

An attack off the Dutch coast.

Right: A view from the observer's cupola of the Strike Wing in action.

skilful leadership brought the attackers into position and the onslaught began.

Despite intense anti-aircraft fire, Wheeler brought the three sections of 236 into dive-bombing the escorts. Sqn Ldr John Holgate of 143 led his men into cannon attacks against the leading minesweepers. Ellis picked out an escort and, with cannons firing, he dived at 20-degrees and released his bombs before escaping from the heavy flak to make his way home.

As the escorts were being hit, the dozen 'Torbeaus', in two sections led by Wg Cdr Charles Cooper and Bill Sise, dropped their Torpex-Duplex torpedoes - set to run at eight feet depth - from 100ft. One hit was seen amidships on the leading merchant vessel, confirmed by the fighter escort, and a second struck the stern of a merchantman, which started to list and turn out of line. The 'Torbeaus' strafed with cannon before departing.

The Assessment Committee (which analysed film, photographs, crew debriefs and enemy radio intercepts) confirmed that two merchant ships, the *Aludra* of 4,900 tons and the *Narvik* of 4,250 tons, had been sunk, together with a flak-ship. Others had been badly damaged. A Beaufighter of 143 Squadron failed to return.

GRIM JUSTIFICATION

Throughout the intensive training period, Wheeler had always insisted that fighter escort was essential. This requirement was grimly justified on May 1 when 31 Beaufighters of the North Coates Strike Wing, led by 'Dusty' Denholm, were sent on a sweep along the Norwegian coast against the cruiser *Nurnberg*. The target was outside the range of fighters and the 'Beaus' approached the Norwegian coast without an escort.

The cruiser was sighted and the Wing had just turned in to attack when Focke-Wulf Fw 190 and Messerschmitt Bf 109 fighters intercepted. Before Sise could get his torpedo-bombers into position, the Germans shot down three of them.

In the melee that followed, torpedoes and bombs were jettisoned, the Beaufighters descended to sea level and turned for home. Two Fw 190s closed in on Del Wright but sheared off to attack another Beaufighter. Wright landed at Skitten in the Orkneys and others went to Wick. In addition to the three lost by 254 Squadron, two machines from 143

> "...THE ATTACKS WERE CAUSING MAJOR DISRUPTIONS TO THE CRUCIAL SUPPLIES OF RAW MATERIALS TO THE GERMAN WAR MACHINE."

also failed to return.

The next strike on May 17 had the benefit of a formidable fighter escort of 59 Spitfires. A Mustang of 2 Squadron had sighted a northbound convoy as it left the Hook of Holland and it was shadowed and photographed by other Mustangs and a raid was ordered. Using the photographs, Wheeler briefed his crews.

At 15:15, he took off at the head of 26 Beaufighters, nine from 236 carrying bombs, six of 143 with cannon and Sise leading 12 torpedo-carriers of 254. Tucked into the leading section of 'Torbeaus' was Del Wright.

By the time the force made contact with the convoy it was off Texel. Six merchant vessels were disposed in two lines, escorted by three 'M-class' minesweepers sailing in front with four armed trawlers on the flanks. All the merchants were flying balloons on a 400ft cable.

Sise, Wright and Plt Off W G Palmer attacked the leading merchant in the starboard column. Others singled out the second vessel and they reported seeing a torpedo hit on Sise's target and the 3,000-ton *Kyphissia* was seen to be on fire. Some of the escorts were also hit and left blazing. Two of the merchant vessels had been seriously damaged and three escorts were damaged.

CHANGE OF FORTUNE

The success of the North Coates Strike Wing started to attract the attention of the RAF hierarchy. Wheeler's tactics were proving that the squadrons were capable of reacting quickly and effectively, once a worthwhile convoy had been reported. On May 27, King George VI and Queen Elizabeth visited North Coates and met the air and ground crews. This emphasised the dramatic turnaround in the fortunes in the six months since Wheeler had assumed command.

Sgt David Ellis with a Tiger Moth.

The 'Hoegh Carrier' taking a beating.

At the beginning of June, Bill Sise was rested. He had established a formidable reputation as a fearless anti-shipping pilot and during his time on 254 he had led almost all the torpedo sections in the face of intense flak.

A few weeks later it was announced that he had been awarded the DSO for: "leading attacks against enemy shipping during which no less than seven large merchant vessels have been destroyed. He has pressed home his attacks undaunted by any danger or opposition."

After a break, he took command of a DH Mosquito squadron and flew out of Portreath in Cornwall against the French Biscay ports. He then joined the Banff Wing when he assaulted heavily defended convoys off Norway. He added another DSO and DFC to his gallantry awards. By the end of the war, he was recognised by many as the RAF's leading 'ship-buster'.

FORMIDABLE CONVOY

Routine for the Wing was to launch two or three aircraft daily to carry out LAGOON sorties along the Dutch shoreline searching for convoys. On June 12 recently-commissioned David Ellis found a small group of coasters off the island of Nordeney, but it was not considered sufficiently important to mount a strike.

However the following day the North Coates Wing was in action with Wheeler once again in the lead. At 20:45 a force of 18 anti-flak Beaufighters and 12 'Torbeaus', this time led by Charles Cooper, took off accompanied by a strong fighter escort. One of 254's aircraft returned early when the radio caught fire – it was extinguished with a tin of orange juice!

The northbound convoy was sighted a few miles south of Den Helder and presented a formidable sight. It consisted of the 5,180-ton *Stadt Emden* and three smaller merchants of 2,000 to 3,000 tons, escorted by five 'M-class' minesweepers ahead and astern of the convoy, with two trawler-type auxiliaries on either flank. All the merchant ships were trailing balloons.

Wheeler sighted the convoy to the north of his route and had to make rapid adjustments to his plan. During the approach phase the formation came under heavy fire and Wheeler ordered the co-ordinated attack, accepting that not all the aircraft were well positioned. He led the anti-flak team against the escorts as the 'Torbeaus' approached the *Stadt Emden,* which had been nominated as the main target.

The torpedo-bombers encountered intense flak and some were badly positioned or baulked on their runs and only seven torpedoes were dropped. Attacking in fluid pairs, Del Wright was one of the pilots who managed to release against the main target, which was hit and swung out of line listing heavily to port.

Other ships were left blazing after being hit by cannon and bombs. It was later confirmed that the *Stadt Emden* and another merchant vessel had been sunk and a number of escorts seriously damaged. One Beaufighter was lost.

ROCKET DEBUT

On June 22, Del Wright took off at 04:20 on a LAGOON reconnaissance and headed for the Dutch coast where he sighted a large convoy of eight merchant vessels and six escorts off Vlieland. Having noted the details, he returned to North Coates.

A Wing strike was ordered and 36 aircraft took off. The 143 and 236 Squadron aircraft were armed with cannons and, for the first time, with rocket projectiles with a 60lb explosive heads.

Thirteen heavily-armed escorts protected the convoy and Ellis dived on one of them, firing his cannon and releasing the rockets at close range. This achieved only modest results with three of the escorts damaged.

Two 'Torbeaus' were lost and three crash-landed on return and others were damaged. It had been a very modest debut for the rocket, but over the next two years, and after some early difficulties, it proved to be outstanding and became the major anti-shipping weapon, eventually replacing the torpedo.

After this difficult operation, North Coates suffered a serious blow when Wg Cdr W O V Bennett, CO of 143 Squadron, was lost with his observer Fg Off H Emmerson. While Neil Wheeler was recognised as the natural leader of the North Coates Wing; he had just been awarded a Bar to his DFC and the other COs also led the on occasions in addition to their own squadrons. In this way, the Wing was not wholly dependent on one man and a number of the senior pilots studied and practiced the tactics.

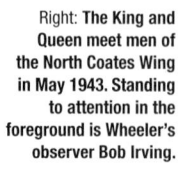

Right: The King and Queen meet men of the North Coates Wing in May 1943. Standing to attention in the foreground is Wheeler's observer Bob Irving.

FIRST OF THE 'TENS'

Towards the end of July, the first of the new TF.Xs arrived to re-equip 236 Squadron. On August 2 they went into action for the first time. A reconnaissance sortie had spotted a large enemy convoy off Terschelling Island. After studying photographs, Wheeler took off at the head of 24 anti-flak Beaufighters and 12 'Torbeaus'. He saw the convoy at 11:35 and positioned his formation.

The rockets performed well and the torpedo-bombers flew in at low level to release as the Spitfire escort fought off a force of Bf 109s attempting to intercept. The iron-ore carrying 2,700-ton *Fortuna* was hit and sank within minutes. An flak-ship exploded and others were damaged.

This final sortie was a satisfying end to Neil Wheeler's arduous and extremely successful time in command of 236 Squadron. Throughout the spring and summer of 1943 he had led numerous successful strikes off the Dutch Frisian Islands, which sank a number of merchant ships carrying crucial raw materials from Scandinavia to Rotterdam.

Within a few days he was awarded the DSO. The citation described him as: "an outstanding leader with cool courage and infectious confidence." David Ellis, one of his youngest pilots, commented: "we considered him to be the father of the Strike Wings and found him a great and inspiring leader." In January 1976, Air Chief Marshal Sir Neil Wheeler GCB, CBE, DSO, DFC* retired from the RAF.

It was time for Del Wright to have a rest and it was soon announced that he had been awarded the DFC. The citation recorded that he had been on continuous operations for over two years and had flown 74 sorties. It concluded: "He has shown himself to be a fearless pilot and his efficiency, keenness and devotion to duty has at all times been a great example to the squadron."

David Ellis remained with the North Coates Wing until the end of the year when he was awarded the DFC after 12 months of 'ops'. After a six-month rest he returned in January 1945 and flew strikes against convoys off Norway.

UNDER THREAT

Losses among the Beaufighter strike wings were some of the heaviest in the RAF and, despite outstanding leadership and gallantry, success rates were relatively low with just 13 sinkings of enemy merchant ships. In part, this was due to a lack of a suitable fighter escort.

Despite the success of August 2, Coastal Command's AOC-in-C, Air Marshal Sir John Slessor, wrote to the Air Ministry six days later saying that he could no longer justify the continuation of the North Coates Strike Wing. He suggested the assets should be transferred for operations in the Bay of Biscay against the increasing U-boat threat.

Not unnaturally, this caused a considerable stir and a meeting was convened on the 20th when senior Air Force and Naval officers met. The C-in-C of Nore Command, which had responsibility for the southern North Sea and off the Dutch coast, strongly supported the Wing as a complement to his other operations. The representative from the Ministry of Economic Warfare presented the most powerful argument indicating that the attacks were causing major disruptions to the crucial supplies of raw materials to the German war machine.

The North Coates Strike Wing was saved. The re-equipment gathered pace and by the end of 1943, new wings had been established at Wick, for operations off Norway, and the 'Anzacs' at Leuchars in Fife. As the war progressed, some moved to new locations and most of the units were re-equipped with Mosquitos that ranged from the Bay of Biscay to Norway. The three North Coates squadrons retained their 'Beaus' and continued the war from their Lincolnshire base until victory in Europe.

No shipping was safe from the rocket-firing Beaufighters and Mosquitos of the Strike Wings. The development and tactics of these potent forces had been pioneered in 1943 by men like Neil Wheeler, Bill Sise, Del Wright, David Ellis and their gallant North Coates colleagues flying from the windswept Lincolnshire coast.

> "AT THE LAST MOMENT, WITH MY SIGHT STILL ON THE SHIP, I RELEASED MY TWO BOMBS AND SKIMMED OVER IT..."

Top: **The 'Hoegh Carrier' ablaze, prior to sinking.**

Above: **David Ellis (left) and his observer Eric Ramsbottom.**
David Ellis

Above, left: **A TF.X of 236 Squadron being loaded with 2in rockets.**

DESERTS and SEAS

Combat over the North Sea was challenging enough, but as its remit expanded Coastal Command faced wide-ranging commitments in the Mediterranean. The first Bristol Beaufort torpedo-bombers became operational in April 1940, dramatically increasing the Command's potential. But it was the prospect of the Beaufighter that really got the 'top brass' salivating; here was a truly versatile strike weapon.

With a range of around 1,170 miles (1,882km) the Mk.I offered phenomenal 'reach' for a fighter; but Coastal Command needed more. Awesome though the Beaufighter's battery of guns was, endurance was more important. It was decided to sacrifice the six machine-guns in the wings and replace them with fuel tanks.

This would take time to achieve in terms of re-engineering and production, so Bristol set about giving Coastal Command an interim 'fix'. A 50-gallon (227-litre) fuel tank as fitted to Vickers Wellington bombers could be squeezed into the fuselage, above the cannon bay and in between the pilot and observer.

The definitive Mk.Ic featured direction finding equipment and a bench for the observer-turned-navigator to plot the long courses the new type offered. Within the wings was an extra 74 gallons of fuel, giving an impressive total of 624 gallons on board. This gave the 'Beau' a maximum range of approximately 1,500 miles. Coastal Command had a fighter that could escort convoys deep into the 'Med' and - thanks to its four 20mm cannon - could inflict considerable damage on enemy shipping and aircraft.

MIXED FORTUNES

During its brief existence in World War One, 252 Squadron operated another twin-engined type, the Blackburn Kangaroo. These biplanes flew patrols off the north east coast from May 1918 until the unit disbanded in June the following year.

No.252 was resurrected on November 21, 1940, at Bircham Newton in Norfolk, under the command of Sqn Ldr Robert G Yaxley MC. Bristol Blenheim Mk.Is and IVs formed the first equipment and some of these stayed on until April 1941.

On December 1, the squadron moved to Chivenor in Devon in preparation to become the first Beaufighter Coastal Command unit and on December 27 R2198 *B-for-Beer* touched down. This was a standard Mk.If intended to get aircrew and groundcrew used to the potent new twin. On New Year's Day R2152 arrived, which had been fitted with

Mk.If R2198 'PN-B' was the first Beaufighter delivered to 252 Squadron and, as Coastal Command's inaugural example, was flown for official photos in December 1940. Bristol

CONVOY ESCORT AND ANTI-SHIPPING STRIKES WERE JUST A PART OF 252 SQUADRON'S REPERTOIRE JONATHAN GARRAWAY RELATES

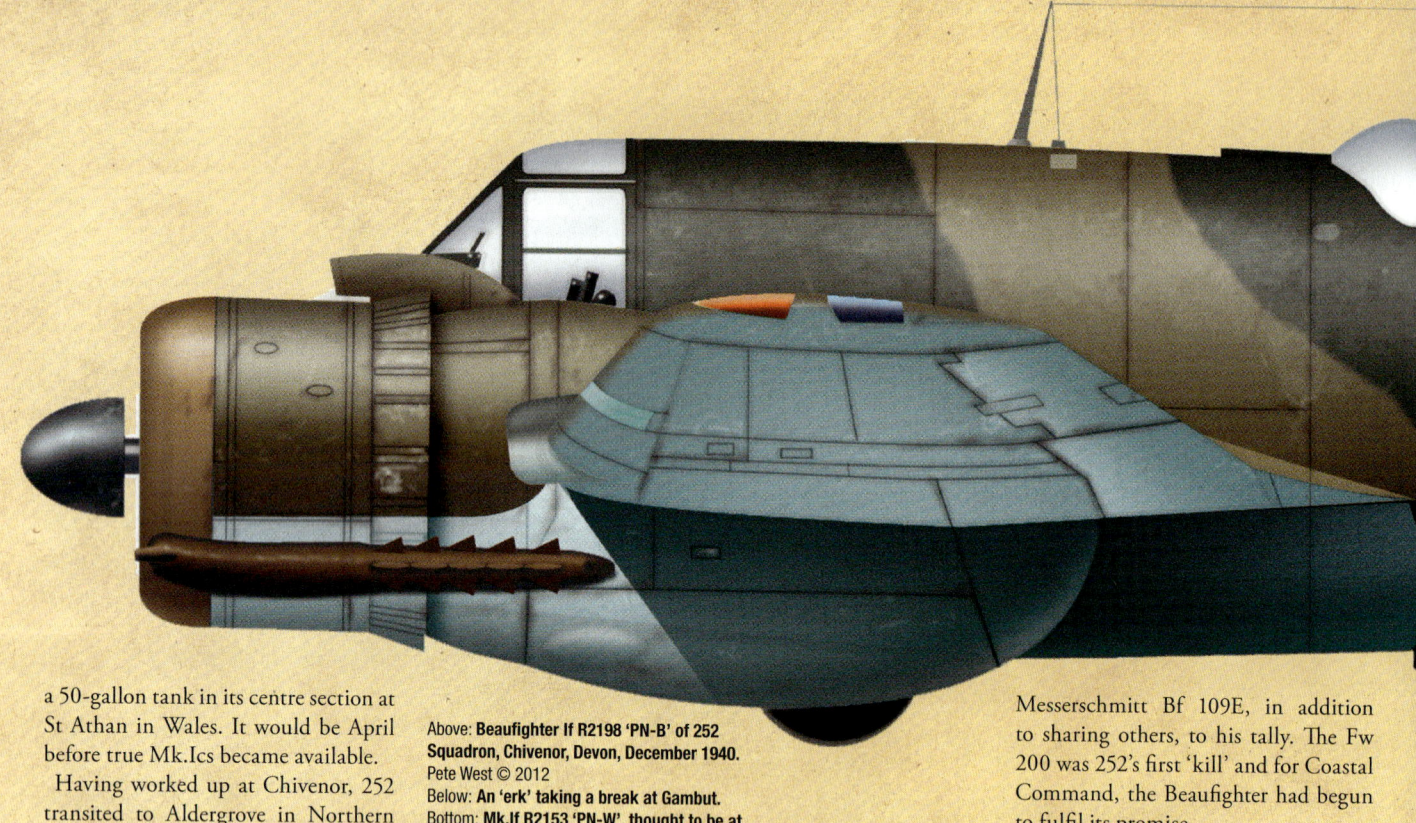

"SUSTAINED BURSTS, ENDING IN A POINTBLANK RANGE ONSLAUGHT, SENT THE CONDOR INTO THE SEA WITH THE LOSS OF ALL ON BOARD."

a 50-gallon tank in its centre section at St Athan in Wales. It would be April before true Mk.Ics became available.

Having worked up at Chivenor, 252 transited to Aldergrove in Northern Ireland on April 6, 1941, and was declared operational. On the 16th, Flt Lt Bill Riley and observer W/O Donaldson in Mk.Ic T3237 *K-for-King* caught a Focke-Wulf Fw 200 of Kampfgeschwader 40 off the coast of Scotland. Sustained bursts, ending in a point-blank range onslaught, sent the four-engined Condor into the sea with the loss of all on board.

Riley had downed a Heinkel He 111 on May 26, 1940, while flying a Gloster Gladiator biplane of 263 Squadron in the Norwegian campaign and during the Battle of Britain, at the helm of Hawker Hurricanes, had added a Junkers Ju 88 and a

Above: **Beaufighter If R2198 'PN-B' of 252 Squadron, Chivenor, Devon, December 1940.** Pete West © 2012
Below: **An 'erk' taking a break at Gambut.**
Bottom: **Mk.If R2153 'PN-W', thought to be at Chivenor in early 1941.**

Messerschmitt Bf 109E, in addition to sharing others, to his tally. The Fw 200 was 252's first 'kill' and for Coastal Command, the Beaufighter had begun to fulfil its promise.

The euphoria of the first victory had to be weighed against the unit's first deaths while flying the Beaufighter that very same day. Plt Off J G Lane and his observer Sgt S Cross both perished when T3238 *S-for-Sugar* was shot down by a Messerschmitt Bf 110 off the coast of Norway.

Three days after the Condor had spiralled into the North Sea, German forces took the Greek port of Salonika. No.252 Squadron was among the assets ear-marked to increase forces in the Mediterranean. The first Beaufighters set off for St Eval in Cornwall, the point of departure on May 1 for the three-day ferry to Luqa on Malta.

ISLAND FORTRESS

On the first leg to Malta on May 1, 1941, Mk.Ic T3229 had to force-land in neutral Portugal; aircraft and crew being interned. (Portugal was later to adopt *functioning* Beaufighters, operating TF.Xs post-war.)

Worse was to come, Flt Lt Riley - of the Fw 200 shoot down - found himself on the receiving end while approaching Malta on May 3. A defending Hurricane

252 SQUADRON AIRCRAFT

Type	From	To	Example
Blenheim If	Dec 1940	Apr 1941	L1279
Blenheim IVf	Dec 1940	Apr 1941	V5816
Beaufighter Ic	Dec 1940	Jun 1941	T4834
Beaufighter VIc	Sep 1942	Jan 1944	JL765
Beaufighter XI	Jun 1943	Jan 1944	JL898
Beaufighter X	Jan 1944	Dec 1946	NT895

From December 1940, 252 Squadron adopted the codes 'PN-' but these were dropped as it deployed to Malta. Once re-established in Egypt, 252 took on 'BT-' but by April 1943 single-letter codes were adopted.

attacked T3237 in error and Riley made a spectacular forced landing at Luqa. He and his observer were injured, but *K-for-King* was a write-off.

Bill Riley was patched up and back in the air by the 7th when 252 was escorting a force of Blenheim IVs on a raid to Sicily. In the middle of this, an Italian Savoia-Marchetti SM.81 Pipistrello tri-motor transport was spotted and Riley, Sub Lt Fraser and the CO, Robert Yaxley shared shooting it down. No.252 was to acquire a taste for three-engined transports...

Three days later, the squadron used the 20mm cannon on its Beaufighters to good effect when they struck an airfield near Catania on Sicily in an early morning raid. Two enemy aircraft were destroyed and five others damaged. On the 17th the unit *detached* to Maleme on Crete and from there struck at German-held airfields in Greece. Such was the tide of war that seven days later, Sqn Ldr Yaxley took 252 to *attack* Maleme, following the German invasion of the island on the 22nd. Eight Junkers Ju 52 transports were destroyed on the ground.

During its time on Malta, 252 Squadron had taken a mauling, with four 'Beaus' failing to return from operations and another quartet

Above: A 252 Squadron Mk.Ic at rest at Idku.

Right: Although built as a Mk.Ic, the blackened shell ejection chutes under wing reveal that T4828 'BT-B' has wing machine-guns.

Above: **Another view of Coastal Command's first 'Beau', R2198.**

Right: **A member of 252's ground crew at work on a Beaufighter at Idku.**

Below: **Beaufighters of 252 Squadron overflying Athens during the victory celebrations, May 8, 1945.**

destroyed on the ground at Luqa. It was decided to wind down the unit, with some personnel going to the UK and others moving to Abu Sueir in Egypt in June. There they worked within the Beaufighter-equipped 272 Squadron until 252 was staffed and equipped sufficiently to operate independently again.

Two aircraft returning from Malta came to grief in very different ways after departing Gibraltar on the morning of May 22, 1941, with St Eval in Cornwall as the intended destination. Mk.Ic T3249, flown by Fg Off S McDonald, with observer Sgt Booth and Fg Off G Lemar as a passenger, ran low on fuel off the Cornish coast and ditched. All three were picked up by a civilian vessel. Fg Off J Holgate in T3235 had no such limitations; he overshot the west country and made a forced landing on the racecourse at Leopardstown in neutral Eire. McDonald, observer Sgt Barnett and 'extra' Fg Off H Verity were interned - but only briefly before finding themselves in Northern Ireland.

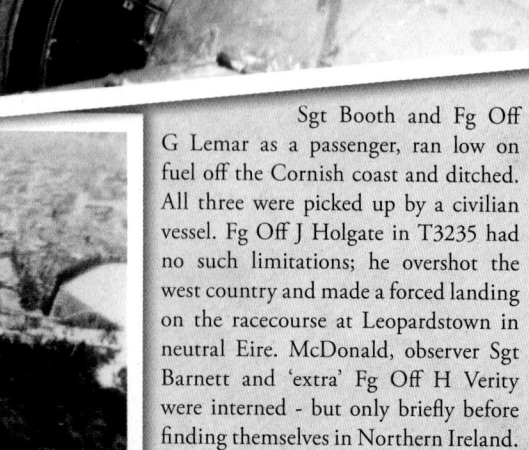

HOME-SPUN 'ACE'

No.252 came out from under 272's 'wing' in December 1941 at Idku in Egypt, with Sqn Ldr A G Wincott taking command from the 22nd. On January 16, 1942 the squadron conducted its first operation and ten days later Fairey-built Mk.Ic T4720 failed to return from a strafing raid on El Agueila in western Egypt.

January brought better fortunes to 252, with sorties into the summer comprising desert strikes and deployments to Malta. On January 18, Plt Off Herbert 'Bert' Horatio Kitchener Gunnis was flying Mk.Ic T4834 *F-for-Freddie* on a convoy patrol off the Libyan coast when he shot down a Ju 88 and had two more added to his score as 'probables'. Sadly T4833, flown by Plt Off Beet, failed to return from this combat. There was much more to come from Gunnis, but *Freddie* had less than a month to go, eventually being destroyed on the ground during an air raid on Luqa on February 15.

On March 11 during a convoy escort off Tobruk, Plt Off A D Frecker shot down two He 111s and Plt Off Smith dispatched a Ju 88. Bert Gunnis sent a Ju 88 and two He 111s into the sea.

The Luftwaffe was desperately trying to re-supply Rommel's forces and its large 'air trains' of Ju 52 tri-motors offered potentially easy pickings. This was the case on May 12 when half a dozen 'Beaus' of 252, escorted by Curtiss Kittyhawks, fell upon 13 Ju 52s escorted by just a pair of Bf 110s. Gunnis, flying *G-for-George*, carried out a head-on attack on one Junkers, sending its down in flames, and damaged another. On return to base, Bert carried out a successful wheels-up landing. This did not dampen the celebrations, for he had notched up five 'kills' and had become an 'ace'.

No.252 brought about the demise of five Ju 52s in that battle, with Sqn Ldr Wincott and Flt Sgt Reg Ivey (in T4831 *D-for-Dog*), taking two each. All together, the Luftwaffe lost *eleven* of the transports (nine were shot down and two force-landed) and one of the Bf 110s. It was not all one-sided: a Ju 52 rear gunner shot down Sgts Cripps and Batemen in T5028 of 252.

In June Bert Gunnis was awarded the DFC and promoted to Flying Officer. The incredible conflict of May 12 brought to an end his air-to-air victories, but he had not lost his taste for tri-motors. On June 28 he and observer Sgt E W Waller caught two more on the ground at Derna in the Libyan desert and they fell apart under his fusillade of 20mm shells, but ground fire ripped upwards and Bert was badly wounded in the legs.

In the cramped confines of the cockpit, Waller managed to patch up his pilot and, with suitable instruction, flew the Beaufighter back to base. Sgt Waller was awarded a DFM while Bert went back to the UK to recuperate. He later became an instructor on 'Beaus' at 132 Operational Training Unit at East Fortune in Scotland.

VERSATILE WARHORSES

Daily taskings for 252's aircrews were varied both geographically and tactically with the second half of 1942 well illustrating this. On July 2, the Beaufighters strafed the airfield at Fuka - the squadron had been based there in late 1941 - and destroyed

252 SQUADRON BASES

Nov 21, 1940	Re-formed at Bircham Newton, Norfolk
Dec 1, 1940	Chivenor, Devon
Apr 6, 1941	Aldergrove, Northern Ireland
May 1941	Luqa, Malta and a detachment at Maleme, Crete
Jun 1941	Abu Sueir, Egypt; crews working initially within 272 Squadron; 252 was essentially a separate unit by Sep 1941 and officially recognised as such in Dec 1941
Nov 1941	Idku, Egypt
	Detachments: El Gubbi, Libya; Berka, Libya; Fuka, Egypt; Luqa, Malta; Paphos, Cyprus, LG.105, Western Desert
Jan 18, 1943	Berka III, Libya
Feb 21, 1943	El Magrun, Libya
	Detachments: Berka III, Libya; Misurata, Libya; Gambut, Libya; Bersis, Libya
Aug 3, 1943	Berka III, Libya
	Detachments: El Magrun, Libya; Gambut, Libya; LG.91, Western Desert
Sep 11, 1943	Limassol, Cyprus
Sep 23, 1943	Lakatamia, Cyprus
Dec 16, 1943	LG.91, Western Desert
	Detachment: Shallufa, Egypt
Jan 21, 1944	Mersah Matruh, Egypt
Feb 6, 1945	Aboukir, Egypt
Feb 10, 1945	Gianaclis, Egypt
Feb 18, 1945	Hassani, Greece
Aug 28, 1945	Araxos, Greece
Dec 1, 1946	Disbanded

Below: A 252 Beaufighter returning to Idku with a signature 'beat up'.

"A DEFENDING HURRICANE ATTACKED T3237 IN ERROR AND RILEY MADE A SPECTACULAR FORCED LANDING AT LUQA."

"EIGHT JUNKERS JU 52 TRANSPORTS WERE DESTROYED ON THE GROUND."

three Bf 109s. This came at a high cost, with two of the attackers going down to the guns of a Bf 109 and an Italian fighter. No.252 was back the following day, hitting the landing grounds around Fuka, destroying or severely damaging up to a dozen Bf 109s and an Italian Savoia-Marchetti SM.79 Sparviero.

From August 9, the unit was back on detachment in Malta and was also operating from Paphos on Cyprus. On the 31st, two more Beaufighters failed to return from 'ops'. In mid-September Wg Cdr P H Bragg became the CO and the pace increased dramatically from October 23 when the Battle of El Alamein started. That month, 252 destroyed four ships and six enemy aircraft; on the 25th it accounted for two Ju 88s and a Dornier Do 24 flying-boat.

In November, 252 received a Beaufighter If; Weston-super-Mare-built X7704 fitted with 40mm cannon for operational trials. As related in the feature on weapons, *Punch*, nothing came of this modification.

On December 6, two 'Beaus' failed to return from a desert strafing attack. The 'Boss', Wg Cdr Bragg was killed and his observer, Fg Off Nichols, was taken prisoner. Sqn Ldr A D Frecker DFC and Fg Off T Armstrong, survived a forced landing in T5045 and set off on a long, and successful, trek back to base. On the 12th, Wg Cdr P B B Ogilvie DSO DFC became CO.

From early December, the unit had been operating from one of several landing grounds around Berka, near Benghazi in Libya, and by the summer

View from a 252 Squadron Beaufighter during a raid on the Greek coastline, late 1943.

Below: Salvaging parts from what is believed to be T4828, which came to grief at Idku on June 25, 1942, when an engine cut on take-off.

Bottom: Stripped out T4989 'BT-Y' which was written off when it swung on landing at Idku on June 6, 1942.

LOSSES OF FIRST SQUADRON MK.ICS 1941

Date	Serial	Circumstances
Apr 16	T3238	Shot down off the Norwegian coast by a Bf 110
May 1	T3229	Missing on flight from St Eval to Gibraltar; interned in Portugal
May 3	T3237	Force-landed at Luqa, Malta, after damage from a RAF Hurricane
May 5	T3228	Shot down during attack on Hassani, Greece
May 15	T3239	Missing, no further details
May 22	T3235	Force-landed in Eire on ferry flight from Gibraltar to St Eval
May 22	T3249	Ditched off the Cornish coast on ferry flight from Gibraltar to St Eval
May 31	T3230	Crashed on approach to Fuka, Egypt
Aug 4	T3247	Ground-looped on landing, Luqa, Malta
Aug 28	T3232	Crashed on take-off from Idku, Egypt
Sep 6	T3236	Struck off charge on Malta - also T3240. Both very likely had been destroyed in raids in May
Sep 9	T3233	Abandoned off the Egyptian coast: out of fuel
Sep 20	T3320	Undercarriage collapsed on landing at Amriya, Egypt
Oct 1	T3243	Struck off charge - likely destroyed in May raids
Dec 5	T3242	Crashed on take-off Edku, Egypt
Dec 31	T3250	Missing off the Libyan coast

of 1943, Berka III became 252's main base. By this time Wg Cdr D O Butler had taken command with Wg Cdr P H Woodruff succeeding him in December 1943.

STRIKING BY MOONLIGHT

From May 1943 the squadron was tasked more and more to hit maritime and coastal targets in the Ionian Sea to the west of Greece and the Aegean Sea to the east. For this, 252's Beaufighters carried bombs under the centre section and the wings. From September, the unit moved to Cyprus, greatly cutting down the 'commute' and increasing the sortie rate, which in October peaked at 224.

Ground strikes on airfields, attacks on all forms of shipping and targets-of-opportunity became 252's bread and butter for the remainder of the war.

Contact with the Luftwaffe became increasingly rare, but on January 31, 1944, a Ju 88 was shot down, but two Beaufighters failed to return.

The following month, the squadron added rocket projectiles to its arsenal, greatly increasing its strike capacity. On June 1, 1944 the Beaufighters ripped into a convoy, sinking a merchant vessel, mauling a destroyer and another ship. South African Wg Cdr Bryce Meharg AFC, CO from March 1944, and his observer failed to return from this action, but lived to fight another day.

Targets in Greek waters and on the mainland remained a high priority for the remainder of 1944, the squadron often using moonlit evenings to its advantage. On October 13 - after a long flight across the Mediterranean - 252 unleashed its rockets on the German fortification at Naxia in Greece and this

Above: **'C-for-Charlie' of 252 Squadron sizzles past the Acropolis, Athens, May 8, 1945.**

Below: **Classic dust storm as a 252 Squadron 'Beau' gets airborne from a desert airstrip.**
All via author

action was instrumental in the Allied capture of the base.

On February 18, 1945 the unit moved into Hassani in Greece and increased the pace of strikes against the retreating Germans. Increasingly there was a new requirement: the harassment of Greece communists as British liberating forces found themselves in the middle of a civil war.

General Montgomery accepted the surrender of German forces at Lüneburg Heath, near Hanover, on May 4 and on that day 252 started an intense barrage of coastal defence artillery positions at Melos in the Aegean. The following day, the last rockets were unleashed and the squadron's valiant part in World War Two was brought to a close. The unit settled on Araxos on the Ionian coast in August 1945 and it was there on August 28, 1945, that 252 disbanded for the final time.

SUBSCRIBE TO
FAVOURITE MA

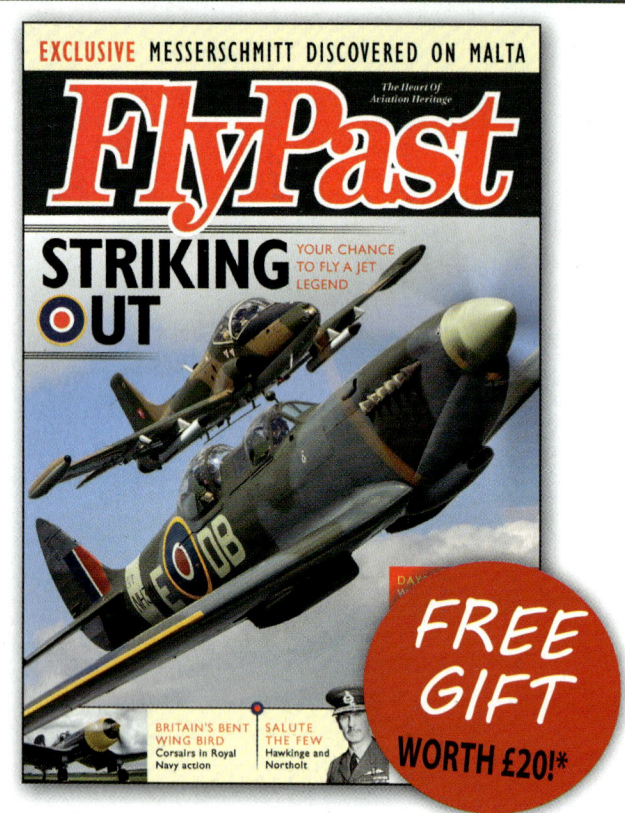

FREE GIFT WORTH £20!*

FREE GIFT WORTH £28.94!*

FlyPast is internationally regarded as the magazine for aviation history and heritage. Having pioneered coverage of this fascinating world of 'living history' since 1980, *FlyPast* still leads the field today. Subjects regularly profiled include British and American aircraft type histories, as well as those of squadrons and units from World War One to the Cold War.

shop.keypublishing.com/fpsubs

Aeroplane traces its lineage back to the weekly The Aeroplane launched in June 1911, and is still continuing to provide the best aviation coverage around. *Aeroplane* magazine is dedicated to offering the most in-depth and entertaining read on all historical aircraft.

shop.keypublishing.com/amsubs

ORDER DIRECT FROM OUR SHOP...
shop.keypublish

OR CALL +44 (0)1780 480404

(Lines open 9.00-5.30, Monday-Friday GMT)

*Gifts subject to change.

551/23

Key Publishing

YOUR GAZINE

SAVE UP TO £23 WHEN YOU SUBSCRIBE!

FREE GIFT WORTH £25!*

Britain at War is dedicated to exploring every aspect of Britain's involvement in conflicts from the turn of the 20th century through to modern day. From World War I to the Falklands, World War II to Iraq, readers are able to re-live decisive moments in Britain's history through fascinating insight combined with rare and previously unseen photography.

shop.keypublishing.com/bawsubs

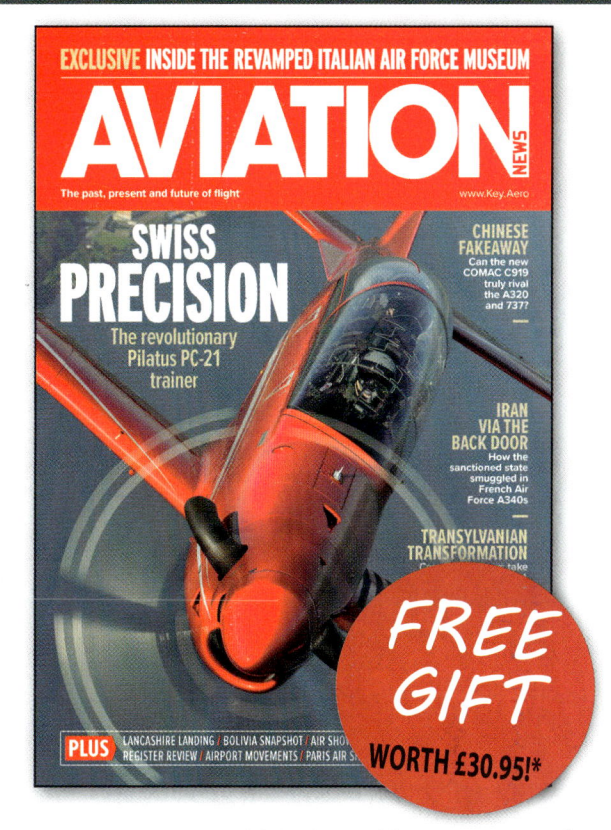

FREE GIFT WORTH £30.95!*

As Britain's longest established monthly aviation journal, **Aviation News** is renowned for providing the best coverage of every branch of aviation. Each issue features latest news and in-depth features, plus firsthand accounts from pilots putting you in the cockpit.

shop.keypublishing.com/ansubs

ing.com

"AS IF GETTING MY AIRPLANE SHOT UP, ENEMY FORMATION AND DUCKING FRIENDL

STARS AND

Bristol Beaufighter VI V8828 'Hi Doc' of the 417th NFS. Pete West © 2012

When the United States became involved in World War Two, the British were well entrenched in the art of night-fighting, as were the Germans. The Americans were initially weak in several areas – and having a combat-ready type was one of them.

It would be May 1944 before the USAAF became operational with its new Northrop P-61 Black Widow. Prior to that, the hard-working Douglas A-20 Havoc was adapted as an interim nocturnal and all-weather fighter under the designation P-70.

In the meantime, there was a war to be fought and a stopgap was needed; one that had already proven itself. In the Mediterranean theatre of operations the choice was the Bristol Beaufighter and, on a very limited basis, the de Havilland Mosquito. Four USAAF units flew in combat in the MTO: the 414th, 415th, 416th and 417th Night Fighter Squadrons (NFS).

YORKSHIRE WORK-UP

After training in Florida, personnel of the 417th took a train-ride to New York in the spring of 1943. There, they boarded the RMS *Queen Elizabeth* for the six-day voyage to the Firth of Clyde in Scotland. From there, they settled into Twinwood Farm, near Bedford.

After a short time, flight crews were checked out on the Beaufighter, which was quite different from the P-70 they had trained on. Radar observers (R/Os) had been using the SCR-540, which did not match up to what the RAF were equipped with – airborne interception (AI) Mk.IV radar, which they now had to get to grips with. Maintenance personnel also had a lot to learn, so the entire 417th was scattered around England at different bases in an effort to get proficient on the 'Beau'.

This intensive familiarisation lasted from May 14 until June 10, during which time the squadron moved en masse to Scorton in Yorkshire where it received a dozen Beaufighters. Scorton was the home base of 604 (County of Middlesex) Squadron, a combat-experienced night-fighter unit flying deadly Mk.VIs.

The 417th continued to train until August 10, by which time the aircrews had accumulated between 70 and 80 hours of night and daytime missions. All of the pilots and R/Os had carried out one or more non-stop cross-countries of between 500 and 1,000 miles (804 and 1,609km) each. All at the 417th knew they would be headed for North Africa.

ALGERIAN BASE

"TAKING A ROUND IN THE FOOT, FACING A HUGE FIRE FROM MY WINGMAN WASN'T ENOUGH!"

STRIPES

THE AMERICANS CAME TO APPRECIATE THE QUALITIES OF THE BEAUFIGHTER IN THE SKIES OF THE MEDITERRANEAN. WARREN E THOMPSON CHRONICLES THE EXPLOITS OF THE 417TH NFS

Early on the morning of August 7, twelve aircrews took off for Tafaraoui, Algeria, by way of Gibraltar. Another six crews went by transport. Appropriately, they were escorted by RAF Coastal Command Beaufighters on the 1,200-mile, six-hour flight. The next leg involved a two-hour flight over to French Morocco and on to their final destination. First duties were mostly convoy patrols, involving both day and night flights, the 417th NFS sharing their base with a French Bell P-39 Airacobra unit.

During the first week of September, the squadron got its first taste of combat with the Luftwaffe when one of the 'Beaus' locked on to a Junkers Ju 88 on a low-level reconnaissance mission. They managed to get some hits but the '88 pulled away and escaped, so it was credited as a 'damaged'.

For the remainder of 1943, there wasn't much activity as the squadron continued to protect numerous convoys. On a few occasions, the Germans attempted attacks on shipping with as many as 20 bombers. The Beaufighters intercepted and turned them back towards southern France, but no 'kills' were recorded.

Victories over the Mediterranean at night were not common for any of the four NFS units in theatre. They had to get closer to the action and, in mid-December 1943, the 417th moved on to La Senia, near Oran, and began to see much more activity.

CHECK YOUR GUNS

On the night of February 1, 1944, Flt Off Rayford Jeffrey and Flt Off Bill Henderson, his R/O, were on convoy cover when they picked up a single intruder coming in low. Jeffrey recalls the action: "We had been on patrol close to the Balearic Islands, Majorca and Minorca, off the coast of Spain. As we started back to our home base at La Senia on the North African coast, I decided to fire my 20mm cannons to check their dispersion pattern. While firing at the water, I noticed that the pattern was somewhat irregular, being angled low to the left.

"My R/O, Henderson, who was stationed in the rear and directly behind the guns (having to cock them manually before engagements) clicked in and observed that we had only 20 rounds left in each of my four cannons and we still had quite a distance to fly before reaching our base. I thought this was pretty wise, so I quit firing.

"Wouldn't you know, about five minutes later I received a call from

...THEY SPOTTED A LARGE FORMATION CONVOY. JEFFREY HAD NEVER SEEN SO

our ground-controller that they had a 'bogey' on radar and they gave me the vector to intercept. The 'bogey' was near Majorca and coming our way. Bill picked it up on his radar and started giving me headings for an intercept. It was just beginning to get light which enabled me to get a visual at about 400m crossing right to left and hugging the surface at approximately 15m right over the water."

"I identified it as a Ju 88. I was at 3,000ft and initiated my attack from the rear and above, closing the range to about 100m. In the darkness, I saw the flashes from the tracer rounds from the turret gunner as he opened fire on me. Aiming just forward of the nose of the 'bogey', I fired a very short burst and saw hits on his cockpit area and down across the wing, inboard of the port engine.

"Suddenly, his port wing separated from the fuselage and the Ju 88 immediately rolled over to the left and dived straight into the water. He was right above the sea so the pilot had no chance to react or get out before impact. I circled above and looked for any survivors but didn't see any. The 'kill' had only used about 10 rounds of ammo from each gun."

For Jeffrey and his R/O, this was their first 'kill' and the 417th's first confirmed victory. Elated, they headed back to base, but trouble was about to start. About halfway back to their base, one of his engines quit and the Beaufighter tried to roll. Apparently, one of the rounds fired by the Ju 88's gunner had hit the engine: the 'Beau' was hard to handle with only one, and there had been several incidents (American and RAF) where it became impossible to maintain altitude. Jeffrey had to fight the controls constantly for the remainder of the flight and, incredibly, was able to make a safe gear-down landing.

WAVE SKIMMING

Ju 88s flying at wave-top height were very difficult to intercept and almost impossible to set up a firing solution. Airspeeds of the two types were about even with the Beaufighter and Ju 88 registering around 300-plus mph.

On March 28, Jeffrey and his R/O were out on convoy escort between the coast of North Africa and the southern coast of Spain. Soon after take-off, ground control radioed that they had a contact on the scope and immediately gave Jeffrey the vector for an intercept. The unidentified 'bogey' was heading straight for the convoy they were protecting.

Jeffrey changed direction and set a head-on course for the intruder. When they were about 20 miles north-east of the convoy, Henderson got a lock-on, and moments later Jeffrey got a visual confirmation that it was another Ju 88 coming straight at them and holding an altitude of only 50ft.

"I started a turn to try to come in behind the intruder, which was difficult due to the low altitude. This was probably one of the Luftwaffe's most versatile aircraft because it was used in a multitude of missions such as bomber, fighter, pathfinder and it was well suited for night work.

"As I tried to get in close, the '88 spotted me and immediately started a 180-degree turn, which was to my advantage because it set me up to easily slide in behind him. I closed to within 250m and opened fire, feeling the drop in airspeed resulting from the recoil of my four cannons. They were firing alternate armour-piercing and high explosive 'ammo'. Most of what I fired missed, but I noticed a few rounds hit him.

"At that time, I saw an object being thrown from the Ju 88. I moved even closer to within 150m, hearing the staccato 'plunk, plunk, plunk' of enemy fire striking my aircraft. Another 'plunk' and I felt the searing heat of a round striking my foot.

"I fired another long burst at him,

Below: The 417th began receiving its P-61s while based at La Vallon, France. Taken from another Beaufighter, Mk.VI V8828 'Hi Doc', with a Black Widow behind, March 1945.
Earl Hissett

THEY MANAGED TO GET SOME HITS BUT THE '88 PULLED AWAY AND ESCAPED, SO IT WAS CREDITED AS A 'DAMAGED'."

"F ENEMY AIRCRAFT HEADING FOR THE
ANY IN ONE PLACE BEFORE!"

exhausting my ammo and was rewarded with seeing parts of the '88 falling from the fuselage – among the them the canopy from the rear gun position that had been firing at me.

"The pilot could no longer maintain altitude and [the aircraft] plummeted the short distance into the water. It didn't take but a few seconds for it to sink at which time I climbed up to 3,000ft and reported to ground control that I had shot the Ju 88 down."

MULTIPLE TARGETS

Ten minutes after his second 'kill', Jeffrey received a call from control that they had multiple targets heading straight for him. At this point, he was flying with his wingman and two RAF Beaufighters. In the distance, they spotted a large formation of enemy aircraft heading for the convoy. Jeffrey had never seen so many in one place before.

Seconds later, the air battle started and Jeffrey noticed tracers coming over the top of his aircraft. He glanced back to find his wingman trying to lob rounds over him to get to the oncoming bombers.

With all of his cannon rounds used up, he relied on his 0.303-calibre machine-guns to fend off the intruders. He spewed out short bursts as he lined up one after another. The two RAF 'Beaus' helped scatter the bombers. Even though none of the friendlies shot down any 'bogies', they managed to turn the entire formation back before they could locate the convoy, so it all ended well. It was time to return to base as darkness was creeping up.

Jeffrey: "I arrived over the base just at dark and found out to my dismay that the enemy gunner had not only knocked out my radar, but also my hydraulic system. This rendered me unable to lower my gear! As if getting my airplane shot up, taking a round in the foot, facing a huge enemy formation and ducking friendly fire from my wingman wasn't enough!

"Now I had to do a gear-up landing and it was dark! I brought her in and hit the ground hard; so hard that one of the restraining shoulder straps broke on impact, instantly dislocating my shoulder. The props immediately stopped and bent as we hit the ground and slid to a halt in a cloud of dirt, dust and grass from the field.

"Once out of the cockpit, I discovered that the round I took in my foot had only entered the thick sole of my flying boot. It was just close enough to my foot to burn it, which made

Right: Crew chiefs precariously perched on 'their' Beaufighter. Note the 'bow and arrow' radar aerial on the nose. 417th NFS Association

Bottom Right: Sgt Steve Perry leaning against his assigned Beaufighter 'Kissimmee Cowgirl', named after a girl met while the 417th was working up in Florida. Richard Ziebart

Left: Maintenance personnel from the 417th NFS in front of a Mk.VI at La Senia, Algeria. Richard Ziebart

Right: The RAF furnished this Hurricane to the 417th for pilot proficiency – all squadron pilots got to fly it. Dan Whitney

Below: Ray Jeffrey's Beaufighter after the gear-up night landing of March 28, 1944. Rayford Jeffrey

me think I had been hit. I still have the bullet to this day."

Intelligence determined that Jeffrey had shot down the pathfinder aircraft that was supposed to have dropped a homing device into the convoy which would have led the rest of the attacking force to the target. That was the object he had seen being ejected from the Ju 88 right after the initial encounter. In an unusual twist, they found out that 25 of the attackers never made it back to base due to battle damage and other reasons.

Jeffrey ended up with one 'kill' and three 'damaged'. Official records stated that the four Beaufighters (two from the 417th and two from the RAF) had engaged and repelled an enemy formation of 70, and had successfully kept them from reaching any of the ships in the convoy.

INKY BLACKNESS

Only a small percentage of missions by night-fighters in the MTO resulted in victories. Countless hours were spent on monotonous patrols when ground control didn't pick up a single 'bogey'. Three nights after dispatching the pathfinder, Jeffrey and Henderson were standing alert at Lapasset, Algeria. Not long into their shift, they received 'scramble' orders and, after getting airborne, were vectored onto an incoming intruder being pursued by an RAF pilot.

Due to the length of the chase, the RAF airman was running low on fuel and was going to have to break off and return to base. Minutes later, Henderson got a lock-on and set up the intercept. As was to be expected, the hostile was coming in almost at wave-top altitude, which made a positive identification difficult.

"We were required to get a visual before firing, and when you are above another aircraft that low over the water you are looking into an inky blackness which was almost impossible to see. The best position to get a 'positive' was from below and, in this situation, there was no way to get under him and if I did, the turbulence from his prop-wash would make it too risky.

"At this point, he began taking evasive action, turning quickly to the right and then to the left. Bill's job was to keep his eyes glued on the screen where he could constantly give me directions so I could keep up with all the Ju 88's manoeuvres.

"The enemy pilot continued to hug the wave tops and I was waiting for him to gain a little altitude and then I would have him. Suddenly, the 'bogey' pulled up enough to fill my gunsight, and I opened fire and saw that my high-explosive incendiary rounds were hitting his wing and fuselage. He pulled up sharply to the right and we lost radar contact. Our ground controller also had nothing on his screen, so we were only able to claim a 'probable'."

Intelligence confirmed that the Ju 88 never returned to its base. A short time later, the British gave Jeffrey credit for three aircraft destroyed and awarded him the Distinguished Flying Cross.

SLIP OF THE PAINTBRUSH?

Cleary visible on the original print, Mk.VI 'Fluff' (below) carrying the serial 'XV912' on the rear fuselage, in Corsica in 1944. USAAF Beaufighters were a rare example of 'Reverse Lend-Lease' and were on loan from the RAF. It was very probably Stoke-on-Trent-built KV912 which is recorded as having been assigned to the 416th NFS. After the USAAF, this machine went on to serve with 600 (City of London) Squadron in Italy. While at 110 Maintenance Unit at Brindisi, Italy, in February 1945 it was written off when it ground-looped on landing and the undercarriage collapsed. Richard Ziebart

Above: An RAF Beaufighter and a Ventura at Tafaraoui along with 417th Beaufighters, late 1943.

Right: 2nd Lt S G Rial (left) and his radar observer, Flt Off J W Chelf, in front of their Beaufighter.

Below, right: A crew chief at the cockpit of a 'thimble' radome-equipped Mk.VI.
All Richard Ziebart

Below: Sgt Richard Ziebart (right) was one of the more experienced maintenance specialists in the 417th Widow eras. Earl Hissett

For the entire tenure of Beaufighters with the USAAF night-fighter squadrons, there was very little, if any, dissatisfaction with the aircraft and most crews enjoyed flying and maintaining it. Its Anglo-American contribution to protecting the ships in the Mediterranean can never be overstated.

"IN THE DARKNESS, I SAW THE FLASHES FROM THE TRACER ROUNDS FROM THE TURRET GUNNER AS HE OPENED FIRE ON ME."

VISIT OUR ONLINE SHOP
TO VIEW OUR FULL RANGE OF **HISTORIC BOOKS**

Key Shop

shop.keypublishing.com/books

NEW

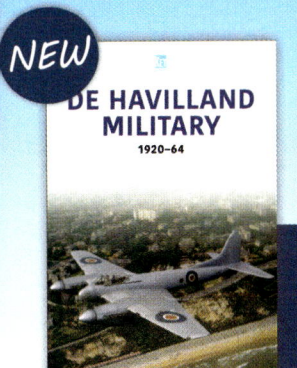

DE HAVILLAND MILITARY 1920-64

Geoffrey de Havilland's contribution to the British aircraft industry was colossal, and many of the aircraft included in this book have remained household names from the day that they first flew. This new book edition of Aeroplane's De Havilland Company Profile 1920–1964 (Military Types) showcases the legacy of one man and his aircraft.

ONLY £16.99

SUBSCRIBERS don't forget to use your **£2 OFF DISCOUNT CODE!**

WELLINGTON – THE BACKBONE OF BOMBER COMMAND

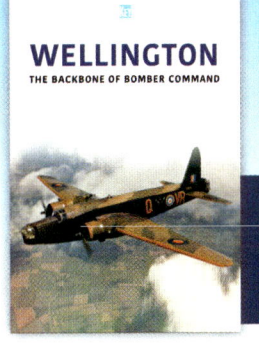

Packed with historic photographs, detailed specifications, eye-witness accounts and manufacturing records, this new book edition of Aeroplane Icons: Vickers Wellington details the history and development of one of World War Two's most iconic bomber aircraft, providing a complete overview of its role in service.

ONLY £17.99

SUBSCRIBERS don't forget to use your **£2 OFF DISCOUNT CODE!**

CONTACT! EARLY US NAVAL AND MARINE CORPS AVIATION, 1911-18
ALAN C. CAREY

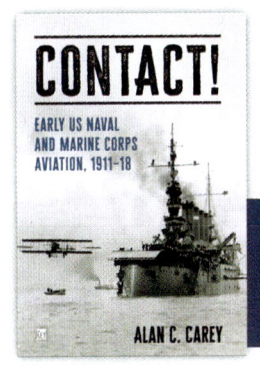

This historical narrative encompasses the formation and development of the US Navy and Marine Corps air services from 1911 to 1918. It includes prewar and wartime training, aircraft development, combat operations, and famous personalities such as Eugene Ely, Glenn Curtiss, Theodore "Spuds" Ellyson, and Alfred A. Cunningham.

ONLY £30.00

SUBSCRIBERS don't forget to use your **£2 OFF DISCOUNT CODE!**

METEOR – FIRST-GENERATION JET FIGHTER

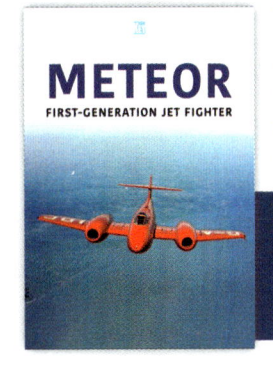

The story of the Gloster Meteor is one of the greatest in the history of the aviation industry and one generally taken for granted. This new book edition of Aeroplane Icons: Meteor tracks the design and development, service and variants of Britain's first jet fighter.

ONLY £16.99

SUBSCRIBERS don't forget to use your **£2 OFF DISCOUNT CODE!**

BLENHEIM – BRITAIN'S FASTEST WORLD WAR TWO BOMBER

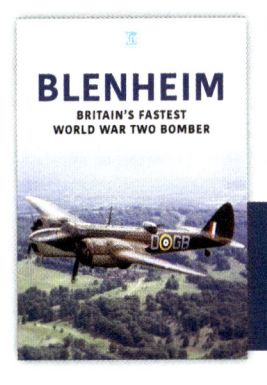

Introduced to RAF squadrons in early 1937, the Blenheim's superb performance made it the RAF's fastest bomber for many years and, before the arrival of the Hurricane and Spitfire, also the fastest aircraft in the entire inventory. This new book edition of Aeroplane Icons: Blenheim showcases this incredible aircraft and celebrates its ground-breaking history.

ONLY £16.99

SUBSCRIBERS don't forget to use your **£2 OFF DISCOUNT CODE!**

SOUTH AMERICAN PROPS
RON MAK

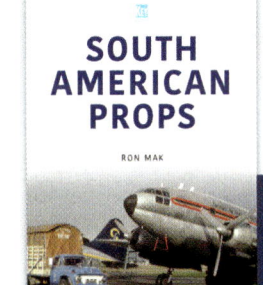

This book details the lifecycles of prop aircraft in South America, including construction, sales, service, repossession, and, on occasion, impoundment. Highly illustrated with over 200 colour images, this book features photos from airports in Venezuela, Suriname, Brazil, Paraguay, Uruguay, Argentina, Chile, Bolivia, Peru, Ecuador and Colombia.

ONLY £16.99

SUBSCRIBERS don't forget to use your **£2 OFF DISCOUNT CODE!**

PRESERVED AIRCRAFT OF THE WORLD – EUROPE
GERRY MANNING

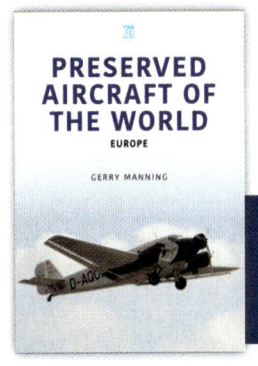

Included in this, the second of three volumes, are a mix of new and old, fast jets, warbirds, bombers, helicopters and vintage light aircraft from around Europe. Some are rare, including prototypes that never made it into production, while others are mass-produced, with pivotal roles in armed conflict, or led the way in commercial flights.

ONLY £15.99

SUBSCRIBERS don't forget to use your **£2 OFF DISCOUNT CODE!**

LUFTWAFFE FIGHTERS OF WORLD WAR TWO
CHRIS GOSS

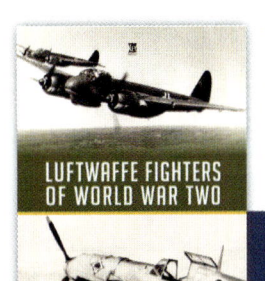

This book gives the reader, be they well-versed in Luftwaffe matters or just simply curious to know more, an insight into the main Luftwaffe fighters of World War Two. The book is richly illustrated throughout with over 200 black and white and colourised photographs and full-colour profiles.

ONLY £18.99

SUBSCRIBERS don't forget to use your **£2 OFF DISCOUNT CODE!**

FREE P&P* when you order online at...

shop.keypublishing.com/books

Call +44 (0)1780 480404 (Monday to Friday 9am-5.30pm GMT)

*Free 2nd class P&P on all UK & BFPO orders. Overseas charges apply.

Night Owls

ANDREW THOMAS DESCRIBES SOME EXPLOITS OF BEAUFIGHTER NIGHT-FIGHTERS

With the Battle of Britain at its height the first Beaufighters were delivered to operational units. The new, heavily-armed, long-range fighters were all destined for night-fighter squadrons. The initial batch was fitted with cannon only but also had the airborne interception (AI) Mk IV radar with its characteristic 'bow and arrow' nose aerials and wing blade aerials. These machines represented a step-change in the nocturnal war.

From the Filton production line, the 'Beaus' were issued to units equipped with Bristol Blenheim Ifs, most of which had been fitted with AI. Getting the Beaufighter ready for its debut were the following squadrons: 25 at North Weald and Debden, 29 at Wellingore, 219 at Redhill and the Auxiliaries 600 at Redhill and Catterick, and 604 at Middle Wallop.

Operations began on September 17 when 29's CO, Wg Cdr S C Widdows, with Plt Off Watson as radar operator, flew an uneventful patrol in R2072. However, the first unit declared operational was 219's 'B' Flight after it had moved to Redhill, and it was one of its pilots who had the distinction of opening the new fighter's account.

On the night of October 2, Sgt Arthur Hodgkinson was airborne near Kenley

"GAVE ONE LONG BURST AT 200 YARDS DEAD ASTERN AND THE ENEMY EXPLODED VIOLENTLY AND FELL INTO THE SEA..."

to the south of London:

"I was vectored out 170 [degrees] and back 350 on to an enemy aircraft [e/a] and I sighted it at about 16,000ft. I observed the enemy flying slightly to my north side ahead of me at a distance of 400 yards. I opened fire at 200 yards – firing approximately 200 rounds in two bursts. I gave a third at 70 yards, but the cannon failed to fire.

"My AI operator observed the e/a dive steeply into cloud. The e/a returned no fire. This aircraft was definitely a Do 17 or 215 as I noticed the humped effect above the forward end of fuselage (where the aerial is) and high wing; also the twin rudders."

Beaufighter If R2101 'NG-R' of 604 (County of Middlesex) Squadron – the mount of the famed night-fighting combination of John Cunningham and Jimmy Rawnsley.
Pete West © 2012

Below: One of the first units to receive the Beaufighter was 25 Squadron at Debden. Note the obsolescent Blenheims behind.
via J D R Rawlings

TEAMWORK AND COMPETENCE

Although 219 Squadron and Arthur Hodgkinson gained the prestige of achieving the first victory, perhaps in the public's perception it was to be the 23-year-old Flt Lt John Cunningham who was the Beaufighter's greatest exponent. Given the nickname 'Cats Eyes' – as much as a cover for the use of the then secret radar as for public morale – it was something Cunningham detested.

John's opinion was that night-fighting was a craft that was a combination of the teamwork and competence of the pilot and radar operator with the ground-based radar technology. This was clearly illustrated on the evening of February 15, 1941 when he and his navigator, Sgt Jimmy Rawnsley, departed Middle Wallop in their Beaufighter heading for the Dorset coast, south of Lulworth. Cunningham had flown Hawker Demons with Rawnsley on 604 (County of Middlesex) Squadron before the war.

Establishing their patrol line at 15,000ft (4,572m) under the 'Starlight' ground control interception (GCI) station, shortly afterwards they were advised that an intruder was inbound at 12,000ft. Cunningham immediately descended to 1,000ft

> "GIVEN THE NICKNAME 'CATS EYES', AS MUCH AS A COVER FOR THE USE OF THE THEN SECRET RADAR AS FOR PUBLIC MORALE, IT WAS SOMETHING CUNNINGHAM DETESTED."

below the enemy bomber in order to silhouette it above them.

They scanned ahead visually. Rawnsley spotted it high and off to port. The night-fighter navigator later wrote:

"John brought the 'Beau' wheeling round on its wingtip. The enemy was a tiny black speck still miles away but incredibly distinct against the opal curtain of light. It must have been a 1,000ft higher than we were and it was coming our way fast, growing bigger and more like a Heinkel every second. I turned to look down-light, trying to see how far he could see in our direction. It was certainly very murky looking that way, with the sea and the sky blending into a dull grey haze.

"The Heinkel was soon high overhead, and John was turning in order to keep vertically beneath it. Apparently they had not seen us and continued serenely on their way. John held his position below them, keeping watch through the roof panel. For a very long ten minutes we continued in company, and all the time it was getting darker.

"But now, all too plainly for my liking, the Dorset coast was showing up. Perhaps the German skipper thought the same thing. The Heinkel went into a slow turn to the right. Steadily John went into a shadowing turn, glancing up and down from the bomber to his instruments."

Their prey was He 111P-2 2911 '1G+FR' of the 7th Staffel of Kampfgeschwader 27 (7/KG27) flown by Ltn Eberhard Beckmann, who orbited it over Lyme Bay until it was fully dark before heading north once more. Cunningham maintained station – then, opening the throttles, closed on the bomber until it was just above them.

Jimmy Rawnsley: "The Heinkel sank slowly into our sights. I waited for the 'hot tomatoes' to come streaming back at us when our guns started their giant pounding. For the first few seconds nothing at all seemed to happen. Then through the choking haze of smoke from the guns, I saw a flash of hits on the starboard engine as John shifted his aim."

At that point the ammunition ran out as the bomber entered a slow descent and Rawnsley, from the navigator's position, feverishly began changing the 60lb ammunition drums. By then Cunningham had lost sight of his target, but the GCI station vectored them in again as the Heinkel headed west along the coast.

Cunningham set off in pursuit, though the target's height made the AI radar unreadable. At 3,000ft, the 604 Squadron crew saw some distance ahead a stick of jettisoned incendiaries explode on the ground – followed soon afterwards by a flash of flame as the Heinkel hit the ground at Higher Luscombe Farm, Harberton.

This was the first victory for the pair when flying together, and the first of ten. They also claimed a 'probable' and two damaged while flying in Beaufighter If R2101 'NG-R' over the next few months.

MEDITERRANEAN PATROL

Proven as a major tool in blunting the night 'Blitz' on Britain, the Beaufighter was later sent in some numbers to the Mediterranean to provide night-fighter defence for the strategically vital island of Malta and the ports of Egypt and the Suez Canal. In March 1943, under Wg Cdr 'Jasper' Read, 108 Squadron was formed at Shandur on the Suez Canal to defend Egypt, Libya and Malta.

No.108 had some very notable pilots including fellow New Zealanders, Flt Lt Victor Verity – who had seven and one shared victories – and Flt Lt Henry Edwards, who had seven. It was over Sicily on the night of April 17/18 that Verity, with W/O Farquharson as his navigator, claimed 108's first success

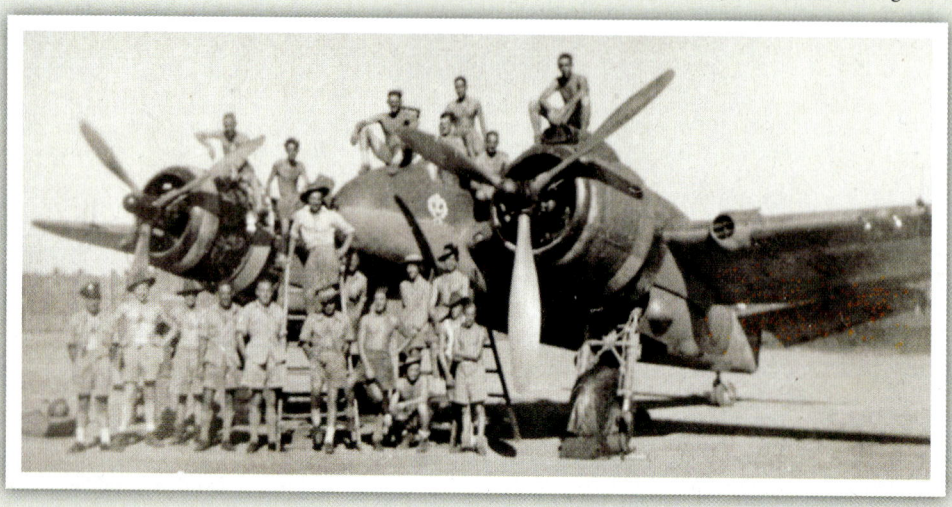

Above: Beaufighter VIf V8708 of 46 Squadron, fitted with a thimble radar dome.
B J Wild

Left: The Beaufighter's first victory fell to Sgt Arthur Hodgkinson of 219 Squadron.
via M Goodman

Below: The Beaufighter's final victory was claimed by a detachment from 176 Squadron which maintained detachments along the Burma front to counter Japanese night nuisance raids.
K R Aunger

when they intercepted a He 111 over Trapani. Verity opened fire and hit the starboard engine after which the bomber spun away and exploded; it was his final victory.

Three nights later a Beaufighter flown by Fg Off Bob Cowper left Malta in the early hours on an offensive patrol to Marsala in Sicily, where he intercepted a Messerschmitt Me 410 which he engaged and damaged. Later, also near Marsala, Fg Off Reg 'Fingers' Foster with Plt Off 'Apple' Newton intercepted Uffz Kohler's Junkers Ju 88C of 10/ZG 26 at 10,000ft. Engaging from 1,000 yards he hit the Junkers in the fuselage and starboard engine and it went down to its destruction.

AEGEAN QUEENS

By 1944 many of the enemy garrisons on islands in the Aegean were dependent on resupply by small coasters, so effective were the air attacks on shipping. In addition the enemy used transport aircraft flying in under the cover of darkness.

In an attempt to interrupt this lifeline, 46 Squadron, headquartered at Edku near Alexandria, sent a detachment to Gambut in Libya in late September. The Beaufighters were to patrol over the Aegean under control of the GCI ship HMS *Ulster Queen*, resulting in an astonishing run of success, the squadron recording officer noting: "Our score of enemy aircraft up to the end of the month is: Destroyed 11 (2 Do 24s, 1 Ju 188 and 8 Ju 52s), Probable 1, Damaged 3."

On the first night of operations, September 26, W/O Roy Butler and his navigator had an eventful sortie by any yardstick. Butler reported: "…sighted two green lights crossing in front port to starboard. I executed a hard starboard turn and closed in to approx 250 yards and recognised a Do 24 flying at 300ft. We attacked from dead astern, gave three short bursts, our third caused flame from the wing. We pulled away to port and watched e/a glide down in flames and crash into the sea, burning for five minutes.

"We returned to control, being vectored to another 'bogey' crossing port to starboard. We obtained contact, decreased to 100ft, closed in and obtained visual on a Ju 52 landplane. Gave one long burst at 200 yards dead astern and the e/a exploded violently and fell into the sea and burned for ten minutes with a huge pall of black smoke.

"Was informed that two further e/a were north and at 23:25 contact was obtained, closed but overshot and target disappeared. Returned to control and was directed to another target and contact was obtained at 2½ miles. Closed in to 100ft, over-shooting and recognised a Ju 52 floatplane. Executed a hard starboard orbit and regained contact at 4 miles range and closed in on e/a 3 miles off the coast of Trypete. Gave one short burst from 250 yards dead astern, observed strikes on e/a starboard engine which caught fire. We followed up with a long burst and broke away hard port, climbing. E/a glided slowly down struck the sea and burst into flames."

Two nights later, Butler and Graham, once more flying in ND243 'Q' (which was named *Kampala Queen* as 46 was the 'Uganda Squadron'), were again successful when they shot down a Ju 188 off the coast of Melos. On the first night of October the pair worked with *Ulster Queen*, as Roy Butler described: "…vectored on to another target coming north at low level. We reduced to 500ft, turned and closed 10 miles west of Melos and recognised a He 111 heading 330 degrees at 250ft.

We opened fire from 200 yards and gave a 3-second burst from dead astern, strikes were observed and pieces flew off the tailplane, fire started in the starboard wing root and smoke poured from the starboard engine. E/a broke away to port and observed to glide down and strike the sea with a small momentary burst of flame and then disappeared."

STEADY HANDS

John Cunningham was engaged as a production test pilot by de Havilland and was a 'weekend wonder' with 604 (County of Middlesex) Squadron when he was called up for active service in 1939. His experiences with DH were compelling and he left the RAF – where he probably would have attained the highest of ranks – to re-join the world of test piloting, the disciplines and teamwork required in night-fighters doubtless contributing considerably to what was now the jet age.

With the death of Geoffrey de Havilland JNR in the tail-less, swept-wing DH.108 TG306 on September 27, 1946 John assumed the role of chief test pilot.

The maiden flight he was most famed for, that of the prototype DH.106 Comet jetliner, was made on his 32nd birthday, July 27, 1949. He was deeply involved in the Comet and Trident programmes and made the transit from DH to Hawker Siddeley in 1963 and to British Aerospace in 1977. He was made an executive director in 1978, retiring in 1980. Gp Capt John Cunningham CBE DSO** DFC* died on July 21, 2002.

John Cunningham, night-fighter 'ace'. KEC

Chief test pilot for Hawker Siddeley, John Cunningham (second left) at Hatfield in early 1965 with the first two Dominie T.1 navigator trainers for the RAF. The aircraft on the right (XS709) joined the RAF Museum at Cosford in February 2011. HSA

Below: A battered propeller blade with 46 Squadron's scoreboard – flanking it is the most successful crew: W/Os Roy Butler (right) and R F Graham. F Baldwin

LAST OF THE MANY

After a long and successful career in the Middle East, 89 Squadron had been sent to the Burma theatre where the Beaufighter remained the primary night-fighter. However, there was little 'trade' for 89 and 176 Squadrons though both maintained operational detachments based close to the front line. In the early hours of March 4, 1945, one of 89's crews had a significant double success.

Just after midnight Beaufighter VIf X8745 – flown by 22-year-old W/O Bert Johnson, an Australian, and his navigator, W/O Chalmers – was scrambled from one of 89's forward bases at Sadaung, just to the east of Mandalay in central Burma, to intercept a Japanese aircraft in the Pakokku area.

As they reached 17,000ft the 'bogey' disappeared and, after orbiting for several minutes, the Beaufighter was directed towards base. Eventually Chalmers gained an AI radar contact crossing from starboard to port at 7,000ft. Johnson turned to come up behind and, closing to 1,500ft, obtained a visual on twin exhaust flames slightly above and to port.

They closed in further, reducing to the target's speed of approximately 140mph (225km/h) until it started to climb, when it was identified as a Kawasaki Ki-48 *Lily* twin-engined bomber. However, as Johnson increased power before opening fire, flames leapt out from a broken exhaust ring at which point the *Lily* saw the 'Beau' and did a wing-over and stall turn to port – closely followed by Johnson and Chalmers who gave a short burst, though without visible result.

The bomber climbed and levelled out when Johnson gave another short volley and the *Lily* went down again with the fighter in hot pursuit. Johnson fired again, hitting the starboard wing, causing pieces to fly off. The *Lily* did one more wing-over to port and levelled out before Johnson hit its port engine, at which point the wing dropped violently and the bomber slipped away with fire coming from the stricken engine. It went over the vertical and headed below the top of the hills and was claimed destroyed.

BACK TO THE FRAY

After landing, the ground crew did well to refuel and re-arm in just 35 minutes. Just before 2am they were off again, as Bert Johnson described:

Opposite, right: **Some of 46 Squadron's very successful Gambut detachment in front of Beaufighter VIf ND243 'Kampala Queen'.**
F Baldwin

Opposite, right: **John Cunningham (right) and his navigator Jimmy Rawnsley (left).**
Peter Green collection

"After an uneventful patrol east and west of Sadaung we were returning to base when we were informed of a 'bogey' 25 miles north at 1,000ft. Given several vectors which successfully brought us behind the 'bogey', which was weaving violently, we increased speed to close-in and contact was obtained at 1,000ft.

"Eventually identified as a *Lily* at 30 degrees to starboard and 10 below, weaving violently, we turned in behind, closed to within 75 yards and opened fire with a long burst. Strikes were seen on its belly from wing root to tail and pieces flew off. Return fire was experienced but no harm was done. The speed of the e/a dropped off very suddenly and it nosed down with flames coming out of its belly. A reflection of the fire was seen on the ground by the observer at approximately 15 miles south east of Mandalay."

This was claimed destroyed, though their victim was actually a Mitsubishi Ki-21 *Sally*. Johnson and Chalmers had taken 89's 'score' to 141 victories. This made it the RAF's second highest-scoring night-fighter squadron.

> **"THE ENEMY WAS A TINY BLACK SPECK STILL MILES AWAY BUT INCREDIBLY DISTINCT AGAINST THE OPAL CURTAIN OF LIGHT."**

ULTIMATE DUCK SHOOT

Flt Lt 'Dickie' Martin, who had been very successful while flying Hawker Hurricanes, flew Beaufighters with 108 Squadron from May to July 1943. Post-war, he became chief test pilot for Gloster and, later, a display pilot for the Shuttleworth Collection. Before his night-fighter stint, he was responsible for an unusual modification to the Beaufighter's arsenal:

"Before I joined 108, I ran the test flight at 107 Maintenance Unit on the [Suez] Canal. There we fitted two 40mm cannon underneath a Beaufighter for attacking submarines on the surface. The first time I fired them (into the Bitter Lake) the mountings broke and did not do the nose of the aircraft much good! However, the mountings were strengthened successfully and the CO ordered the armourers to remove the bullet heads from the cartridges and fill them with No.6 shot. He then proceeded to slaughter huge numbers of ducks on the lakes at Edku!"

Fourth prototype R2055 fitted with Rolls-Royce and Vickers 40mm cannon. via J D Oughton

THE LAST HURRAH!

Almost three weeks later it was the turn of 176's detachment at Akyab, there to counter Japanese small-scale night nuisance raids. On the evening of March 25, 1945 at a little after 10pm, Fg Offs J I H Forbes and H J Pettridge were scrambled and flew south.

No.176's operational record book: "They were vectored to the west of Ramree Island for 1½ hours and were finally vectored onto a low flying 'bogey'. Forbes closed to 200ft below and identified the bandit from plan view as an *Oscar* [Nakajima Ki-43], so he dropped back to 300ft slightly low and gave a short burst. Hits were observed all over the fuselage and a large explosion enveloped the starboard mainplane. The *Oscar* dropped away to port and faded from the AI tube. The interception took place over the coast and the *Oscar* may have gone into the sea. Claim one destroyed."

In the humid tropical skies off the Burma coast, half a world away from the Home Counties where its first victim came down, Forbes and Pettridge's success became the Beaufighter's final victim.

Left: Egypt-based 108 Squadron had a number of successful crews including Fg Offs Reg 'Fingers' Foster (left) and Maurice 'Apple' Newton (right). via C F Shores

Below: Beaufighter VIf X7898 'G' was flown by W/Os Bert Johnson and M Chalmers on their first operation with 89 Squadron in late January 1945. via J D R Rawlings

TT.10 SR912 showing off its yellow and black markings while towing a sleeve target while with the Kai Tak Station Flight, Hong Kong, circa 1952. The sleeve is only slightly deployed for the purposes of the photo, normally it would be a long, long way behind! *Peter Green collection*

TUGGING AT SLEEVES

POST-WAR THE BEAUFIGHTER REFUSED TO RETIRE; DOUG HALL EXAMINES ITS SECOND CAREER WHICH LASTED UNTIL 1960

After such an incredible war, the mighty Beaufighter was destined for a rapid and wide-sweeping stand down. Battle-hardened night-fighter, torpedo bomber and a strike weapon of awesome capability, it seemed that there was little use for the big Bristol with the advent of peace.

It was not just that the need had drastically shrunk but the layout that had made the twin so opportune when it first entered service in 1940 was working against it five years later. That slim fuselage was not capable of taking more advanced airborne interception gear and the remoteness of the gunner-turned-radar operator did not help. The de Havilland Mosquito was to be the night-fighter of choice for the immediate post-war period.

For torpedo-toting and strike attacks another Bristol type, the Brigand, was gearing up for service. For a variety of reasons, that machine was going to prove a disappointment, but as VJ-Day was celebrated on August 15, 1945, all of this was in the future.

When the atomic bombs shattered Japanese willpower, there were just seven frontline Beaufighter TF.X squadrons; two each in India and the UK, and one in Burma, Greece and Singapore (see the panel) plus ancillary and training units. Of those, the last disbanded in October 1946. Like many other warhorses, some 'Beaus' were headed for new lives as instructional airframes, rework and export but most of them were destined for the scrapheap.

NEW LIFE

There was life in the powerful twin yet; benefits were still to be had from the Beaufighter. In the Far East it had the edge over its more nimble de Havilland rival, the Mosquito. The latter's bonded ply wooden structure suffered in extremes of temperature and humidity, while the all-metal Beaufighter could shrug off such privations. Here was a niche for the robust type's operational capabilities.

The good turn of speed and endurance combined to make it very well suited for gun laying and target-towing. All three services had an insatiable need for gunnery practice, even in times of operational cuts. While the fuselage had its restrictions in terms of radar, it could take a winch for pulling gunnery sleeves with ease. The airframe

The prototype TT.10 conversion, NT913, at Filton, with Bristol 170s and Brigands in the background. Note the winch in the upright position and the wire guards around the tail surfaces. Bristol Aeroplane Co

TT.10 RD761 starting up ready for the last-ever RAF Beaufighter sortie at Seletar, May 12, 1960. KE

could take plenty of knocks and was simple to repair. We shall return to the Beaufighter tug – the last of the breed.

For the renaissance of the Beaufighter as a ground-attack platform and in its new role as a surrogate target, a highlight of its character played a part. The Bristol Hercules radial, particularly in the form of the 1,770hp (1,320kW) Mk.XVII powering the Mk.10s was very reliable, plenty were held in reserve and there were vast stocks of consumables. (RAF designations changed from Roman numerals to Arabic in 1948.) Later versions of the Hercules were powering Handley Page Hastings, Vickers Valettas, Varsities and Vikings, so there was a large pool of personnel used to working on them. All of this boded well for the Beaufighter's longevity.

While most of the Beaufighter's 'second wind' was in the support role, its ability to bring devastating amounts of weaponry down on spot targets was still in demand.

In Burma, 27 Squadron was based at Mingaladon and its TF.Xs continued to be involved in 'contact patrols' - shadowing the army as it moved through the undergrowth locating, isolating and capturing straggling Japanese troops.

Despite the surrender, getting the word through to out-of-touch units meant that, occasionally, 'contact' was required and a burst from the guns of a Beaufighter often helped to quell resistance. To further this, 27 dropped over 250,000 leaflets explaining that World War Two was a thing of the past.

Having endured the Japanese occupation, on the island of Java the Indonesian nationalist Achmed Soekarno seized his moment to declare independence from the previous occupying power, the Netherlands, although militarily, the area was a UK responsibility. Britain had enough territorial struggles on its hands and sought to leave Soekarno to deal with the Dutch, while UK forces rounded up Japanese troops and, most importantly, got prisoners of war out safely. But one occupying force looks much like another and from October 1945, British troops were being fired upon. The 'peace' had not lasted long; the UK was unwillingly immersed in what would become the bitter struggle for Indonesian independence.

Among other assets, 27 Squadron was detached to Kemajoran on Java. The Beaufighters transited south through

Based at Llanbedr, Wales, TT.10 SR914 of 5 Civilian Anti-Aircraft Co-operation Unit, at low level in early 1950. It ended its days on Malta in late 1959.
Bristol via Andrew Thomas

TT.10 RD761 of the Seletar Station Flight, May 1960.
Pete West © 2012

Malaya to the new base, arriving in November 1945. They went straight into action and in the space of three months, undertook over 300 'ops'. Many of these were a matter of merely showing up, others involved leaflet dropping, but when close support was required, the Beaufighters were not found lacking. No.27 returned to Mingaladon in January 1946 and disbanded the following month.

EFFECTIVE STRIKE POWER

In Malaya, the huge jungle peninsula behind Singapore spreading up to the Thailand/Burma border, insurrection was fomenting and by early 1948 communist dissidents were becoming more organised. Following a slaughter of plantation owners and staff in Perak, a state of emergency was declared on June 17, 1948. With typically British understatement, what was to become an 18-year conflict became known nonchalantly as 'The Emergency' and in military-speak as Operation FIREDOG.

The nearest heavy strike unit in the Far East Air Force was 84 Squadron at Tengah in Singapore. Previously a Mosquito FB.6 operator, it re-equipped in November 1946 with Beaufighter TF.10s. A detachment was sent to Kuala Lumpur in July 1948. Across the Indian Ocean at Negombo in Ceylon, 45 Squadron traded in its Mosquito FB.6s for TF.10s in December 1946. It too was put on standby and had a flight of 'Beaus' in place at 'KL', as it was known, a month after 84 and the whole unit settled there in May 1949.

Between these two, an average of eight Beaufighters was on call to hit what were called Communist Terrorist (CT) bases, supply lines or even bands of insurgents on the march. Until the arrival of the hard-hitting Bristols, Supermarine Spitfire FR.18s equipped with under-wing rocket-projectiles (RPs) were the first responders. In August an electric fault caused an RP to launch from a Spitfire on the ground and a civilian was killed. This put paid to using the single-engined fighter for strikes but they could still make their presence felt with 20mm cannon.

So 45 and 84's Beaufighters came into their own. Author Robert Jackson in his masterful *The Malayan Emergency and Indonesian Confrontation, The Commonwealth's Wars 1948-1966* (Pen & Sword 2008) summed up the Bristol's advantages: "With its

BEAUFIGHTER TF.X FRONTLINE UNITS AT VJ-DAY, AUGUST 5, 1945

Squadron	Based	Disbanded
22	Gannavaram, India	Sep 30, 1945
27	Mingaladon, Burma	Feb 1, 1946
89	Seletar, Singapore	May 1, 1946
217	Gannavaram, India	Sep 30, 1945
252	Araxos, Greece	Dec 1, 1946
254	Thorney Island, UK	Oct 1, 1946
287	West Malling, UK	Jun 15, 1946

powerful armament of four 20mm cannon, six 0.303 machine-guns, eight RPs or two 250 or 500lb bombs, each Beaufighter was the offensive equivalent of two Spitfires."

The first strike was on August 12 on a camp near the Thai border, where a large concentration of CTs had been found – 30 are believed to have been killed in the first salvoes. Five days later came the biggest strike yet, with Beaufighters supplemented by Spitfire FR.18s. The nature of jungle warfare was such that only one CT was killed in this conflagration.

No.84 left for Tengah in November and from there flew its Beaufighters to Habbaniya in Iraq, where it was to start working up on Brigands. In December 1949, 45 Squadron relocated to Tengah and also started coming to grips with Brigands.

It did not forsake 'Beaus' totally until February of the following year. Because of that, on February 7 Beaufighters were brought in for a strike on a settlement in Johore – the Malay state neighbouring Singapore. Sadly, five civilians were injured and a revision of just how a strike could be called was instigated. This sortie was the last time a 'Beau' was used in anger.

ADDING A THIRD PROPELLER

As mentioned earlier, the TF.10 was regarded as an ideal candidate for conversion to a target-tug. The prototype was NT913 which was converted at Filton in May 1948 and given the designation TT.10.

At least 35 were transformed to the new role up to 1950. The type became an exceptional hard-worker, serving extensively in the UK, the Mediterranean (with the Fleet Air Arm and well as the RAF), the Middle East and Far East.

A winch was placed within the rear fuselage, towing a sleeve via a lug under the tail. The winch was powered by an airstream-driven propeller on a fixed arm extending from the starboard mid-fuselage. When not in use, this propeller was rotated through 90-degrees, so as to create the minimum possible amount of drag. Guards and wires protected the tail surfaces and tail wheel from the tow wire.

A look through the *Beaufighter Squadron Directory* will give details of the eight (including one Royal Navy and one RAAF) full-blown units that operated tugs examples. By 1951 all but 30 Squadron RAAF had disbanded – see the panel for more on the Australian TT.21.

Final 'frontline' RAF squadron to operate the Beaufighter was 167 which

Below: **TT.10 RD761 during its farewell flight around Singapore landmarks, May 12, 1960.** RAF Changi via KEC

AUSTRALIAN TUGS

Australia also turned some of its Beaufighters into target-tugs, the type serving through to 1956, mostly with 30 Squadron. A number, perhaps as many as ten, Department of Aircraft Production-built Mk.21s – the equivalent of the RAF's Mk.X – were converted to similar status as the British TT.10, but without the fin fillet. Illustrated is TT.21 A8-350 wearing a scheme very close to its British counterparts. The first TT.21 conversion, A8-265, wore an overall yellow with black diagonal stripes. **Photo:** Peter Green collection re-formed at Abingdon, Oxfordshire, on February 1, 1953 from 3 Ferry Unit. The outfit existed to fly various types long distances to new 'clients' and with TT.10s in use in all points east to Hong Kong and Singapore, a 'Beau' or two was on strength to keep pilots current. Many second line units flew the yellow and black striped tugs – more details in the panel.

FINAL FLING

During the 1950s and 1960s the Far East witnessed a series of 'last ever' flights. This is not surprising as the RAF tended to post the more 'experienced' aircraft out there, leaving the newer types to bear the brunt of the 'Cold War' in Europe and the Middle East.

In May 1955, 45 Squadron retired the last of its superb de Havilland Hornet F.3 twin-engined fighters at its base at Butterworth, Malaya. Sadly, none have survived through to today, all languishing on the scrap dump.

On May 15, 1959 Seletar on Singapore witnessed the final official flights by Short Sunderland MR.5s. The operating unit was 205 Squadron and the occasion was not just the last of a type, but of flying-boats in the RAF.

Seletar was the venue for the finale of the Beaufighter. This was TT.10 RD761, on charge with the Station Flight, which provided a variety of services for the RAF, Army and Royal Navy stationed at Singapore.

TT.10 RD761 was typical of the tugs. It was built at Weston-super-Mare in 1945 as a TF.X but never saw 'sharp end' service and was stored. After conversion in late 1948 it went off to serve in the target facilities' role with 17 Squadron at Chivenor, Devon; 5 Squadron at Llandow, Wales, and 226 Operational Conversion Unit, also at Chivenor. It was ferried out to the Far East in 1955, joining the Seletar Station Flight.

On May 12, 1960 flying RD761 Fg Off H Marshall made the RAF's final sortie and the last flight of a Beaufighter – until such time as The Fighter Collection's example at Duxford amends the records!

Official photos of this last flight are dated May 16 and this is often quoted in sources. This was the release date of the prints, not of the event!

Eight days later, RD761 was struck off charge, stripped of spares and its forlorn carcass left on the scrap dump. Like 205's Sunderlands and the Hornets of 45 before that, none of the Seletar 'Beaus' found their way into a museum.

BEAUFIGHTER TT.10 NON-SQUADRON USERS

Armament Practice Camps: No.22 Ranchi, India; No.26 Nicosia, Cyprus; No.27 Butterworth, Malaya
Civilian Anti-Aircraft Co-operation Units: No.1 Hornchurch, Essex; No.2 Little Snoring, then Langham, Norfolk; No.3 Exeter, Devon; No.4 Llandow, Wales and later amalgamated with 3 CAACU; No.5 Llanbedr, Wales
Communications and Target Towing Squadron: Luqa and then Ta Qali, Malta
Operational Conversion Units: No.226 Molesworth, Hunts, then Bentwaters, Suffolk, and Driffield, Yorks; No.229 Leuchars, Scotland then Chivenor, Devon; No.236 Kinloss, Scotland
Station Flights: Changi, Singapore; Kai Tak, Hong Kong; Seletar, Singapore
Target Towing Section: Shallufa, Egypt
Target Towing Unit: Abyad, Sudan

Bottom: **TT.10 RD850** served with 229 OCU at Chivenor before moving on to Nicosia, Shallufa and finally Malta; retiring in late 1958. Key Collection

RD761 lifts off at Seletar for its moment of history. KEC

> "It was a real blacksmith's job. You could lose an engine and it would still fly... The manner in which they soldiered on with the minimum of servicing in the Middle East was amazing... The secret of the success of the 'Beau' - especially as a night-fighter - was without doubt our ground crews; these were the boys who should have had the glory and the glamour, not us."

W/O W G Hood, navigator, 255 Squadron

A well-known posed piece of 'fighter' crews and the Rock of Gibraltar. The aircrew and the Beaufighter II were actually from 779 Squadron, Fleet Air Arm, a Fleet Requirements Unit for the passing 'trade' of the warships of the Royal Navy. KEC